Understanding Contemporary Cuba in Visual and Verbal Forms

UNDERSTANDING CONTEMPORARY CUBA IN VISUAL AND VERBAL FORMS
Modernism Revisited

Max Dorsinville

Caribbean Studies
Volume 17

The Edwin Mellen Press
Lewiston•Queenston•Lampeter

Library of Congress Cataloging-in-Publication Data

Dorsinville, Max, 1943-
 Understanding contemporary Cuba in visual and verbal forms : [modernism revisited] / Max Dorsinville.
   p. cm. -- (Caribbean studies ; v. 17)
 Includes bibliographical references and index.
 ISBN 0-7734-6576-6
 1. Cuba--In literature. 2. Literature, Modern--20th century--History and criticism. I. Title. II. Caribbean studies (Lewiston, N.Y.) ; v. 17.

PN56.3.C83D67 2004
809'.327291--dc22

2003066516

This is volume 17 in the continuing series
Caribbean Studies
Volume 17 ISBN 0-7734-6576-6
CaS Series ISBN 0-88946-470-7

A CIP catalog record for this book is available from the British Library.

Front cover photo: *A foggy morning in Santa Clara*. Photograph by Max Dorsinville.

Copyright © 2004 Max Dorsinville

All rights reserved. For information contact

 The Edwin Mellen Press   The Edwin Mellen Press
 Box 450   Box 67
 Lewiston, New York   Queenston, Ontario
 USA 14092-0450   CANADA L0S 1L0

The Edwin Mellen Press, Ltd.
Lampeter, Ceredigion, Wales
UNITED KINGDOM SA48 8LT

Printed in the United States of America

This book is for Roger Dorsinville (1911-1992)

Table of Contents

Foreword — i
Preface by George Lang — ix
Acknowledgments — xiii
Introduction — 1

Chapter One: The Nature of the Look: Garcia's *Dreaming in Cuban* — 17

Chapter Two: The Body as Metaphor: Garcia's *The Agüero Sisters* — 27

Chapter Three: Phenomenology and Photography: *Looking Cuban* — 33

Portfolio — 41

    --Havana — 43

    --Santa Clara — 45

    --Matanzas — 47

    --Back to Havana — 49

Chapter Four: The Body of the Fisher-King: Hemingway's *The Old Man and the Sea* — 51

Chapter Five: Looking for the Light: Walcott's *Collected Poems* and *Omeros* — 59

Chapter Six: Carnival in the Waste Land: Iyer's *Cuba and the Night* — 89

Chapter Seven: Carnival in Greeneland: Greene's *Our Man in Havana* — 101

Chapter Eight: The Gaze of the Unreliable Narrator: Desnoes's

Inconsolable Memories   111

Chapter Nine: Seeing the Light: *Elena and her Friend*   123

Conclusion   131

Appendices   137

    A. *Nationalism and Consumerism*   139

    B. *Declaration on Art and Revolution in Cuba*   159

    C. "*Understanding Contemporary Cuba in Visual and Verbal Forms* from a Haitian Perspective," by Marie-Hélène Laforest   163

Bibliography   169

Index of Names Cited   179

Foreword

Understanding Contemporary Cuba in Visual and Verbal Forms evolved in stages from my experience of living in Cuba. The idea of preserving that experience led to the use of photography, followed by a probing of texts in phenomenology, photography and literature linked by the concept of the *gaze* (the first and lasting experience that struck me about Cuba, the way people looked at you insistently). I relied on these texts to articulate a reflection based on modernist theory. To paraphrase T.S. Eliot's *Notes Towards the Definition of Culture*, my critical tools were set towards an understanding of contemporary Cuba in visual and verbal forms that meant more than what they seemed.

As described in the Introduction, my initial motive for going to Cuba was a release from the written word. It momentarily meant distancing myself from academic work. Once distance was achieved and preserved by means of photography, I turned to writing with the aim of understanding the delayed meaning of what I saw reflected in the people and events in Cuba. Aware of Antonio Benítez-Rojo's description of the carnivalesque mode of Cuban culture (*The Repeating Island* 29), I found that it perfectly matched my quotidian experience. Thus the Introduction was set in the form of a phenomenological reportage centered on people and events that left an imprint on my senses before I was able to understand their meaning.

I am indebted to Jean-Paul Sartre's *Being and Nothingness* and Maurice Merleau-Ponty's *Phenomenology of Perception* for their theorization on the *look*, or the *gaze*, identified as agency in the existential coming to terms of self and otherness. Starting from the commonplace observation that the look is a mute exchange between individual onlookers, Sartre and Merleau-Ponty agree with Joseph Conrad who, in his Preface to *The Nigger of the 'Narcissus'*, considers that the look is more than the exercise of one sense but also a metaphor for a mode of perception associated with intellectual understanding.

Looking at the photos, thinking about what called for a reconciliation of sense and thought, I realized how the double meaning of the look fitted my own experience. Once I wrote down a first draft, I mulled over the unsuspected truth of following in the footsteps of Conrad's Marlow into an unknown, metaphorical darkness with, at one end, the knowledge that half a million Haitians had been granted Cuban citizenship when the Revolution came to power --and meeting with Sixto, a descendant of those Haitians who had preceded me to Cuba-- and, at the other end, a vision of light that meant a redefinition of the notion of identity.

Though Sixto, a retired soldier of the Cuban army, was not Kurtz and nowhere was there an "Intended" (*Heart of Darkness* 84) to whom I was to deliver a message, I returned to North America to tell of a journey that humbled my certainties. I moved from an Outer station to an Inner station where I met my double in the eyes of a Cuban customs officer, whom I left thinking, "But for the grace of God it could have been me... the one he thought I was." And it seemed that every Conradian image I could think of took an added meaning: *fog, haze, mist, river, light, darkness, wilderness, mystery, mission, one-of-us, no restraint, rumours, brooding, power*...[and to crown it all] *"'but heavens! how that man could talk. He electrified large meetings. He had faith --don't you see?-- he had the faith....' "* (115).

Joseph Conrad wrote in the age of Empire. He set his characters on journeys to South America, Africa and Asia; and he told tales of reversibility; i.e. no truth is fixed and unchanging when clearsightedness is achieved. The world his characters journeyed in was phenomenological and not ethereal, or fixed by any man-made construct. From the start of my reflection, Joseph Conrad's thinking, like Benítez-Rojo's, Sartre's and Merleau-Ponty's, was an essential reference.

* * *

The *look* dominated my sensory world of experience in Cuba because of the perceived mode of exchange between a visitor like myself and the people whose guest I was. Looking at the Cuban people and their culture meant their looking at me, in turn, and, rightly or wrongly, their look let me know I was one of them.

Conceptually, the look raised the larger issue of self and otherness I was familiar with in my reading and teaching of modern classics and their philosophical underpinning. Reflecting on Conrad, Sartre, Merleau-Ponty, Camus, Berger and other writers within the mainstream modernist tradition, the first point that came to mind was precisely the fallacy embedded in an unquestioning acceptance of commonality based on appearance; i.e. the initially comforting and reassuring perception of "feeling at home" in a society whose majority population shared my African heritage (hence the phrase repeatedly heard, "You look Cuban"). The second point, related to the first, was my awareness that superficiality was the dead-end awaiting me if I did not reflect on photography, as an art form of surfaces, and phenomenology, as the study of surface phenomena, and consequently probed literature dealing with Cuba with Hemingway's "iceberg theory" prominently in mind; the distinction between the appearance of things and what lay beyond appearance.

There was a substantial existentialist literature on the fallacy of commonly shared categories of language, race, nationality, geography and history starting with Joseph Conrad and developed all the way to Camus and his successors. In all cases, the established categories came up short. I could not but foreground my intended writing about Cuba with a reminder of what Conrad showed in *Heart of Darkness*, West in *Miss Lonelyhearts*, Sartre in *La Nausée*, Faulkner in *Light in August*, and Camus in *L'Etranger*: that a central dilemma of modernity was precisely the absence of conventional markers of identity in a world where the individual was faced with the task of self-invention or re-invention. I understood that a reflection on Cuba entailed joining the mainstream of modernity's interrogation in light of the omnipresence of the uncertainties of displacement, fragmentation and abrogation.

I turned to imaginative works familiar to me that happened to be written by authors who had two things in common: their works centered on modern Cuba, and the attention they paid to the imagistic interweaving of form and substance placed them in the Euro-American modernist literary mainstream. As I proceeded with my thinking and writing about Cristina Garcia, Ernest Hemingway, Derek Walcott, Pico Iyer, Graham Greene and Edmundo Desnoes, it seemed to me that their different perspectives as virtual or actual outsiders shed a prismatic light on the concept of the look and Cuba. Their works seemed to reflect what T. S. Eliot called "a heap of broken images" (*The Waste Land* I.22). Their otherness meshed with mine and inspired the design of this book.

My chosen literary sources and myself never were (or no longer were) Cuban citizens. We were all visitors or temporary residents of Cuba with a view unblinkered by *a priori* categorizations. Yet, I had to consider whether the perspective of the "outsider," for all its merits, was not biased or restrictive when measured against the so-called "native" writer's.

I pondered that question as I remembered reading Alejo Carpentier, Nicolas Guillén, Roberto Fernández Retamar, José Lezama Lima and others. I enjoyed and admired their works; but their perspective was precisely that of the insider who wrote within a tradition that privileged nativeness mixed with the Baroque and magic realism particular to Latin American aesthetics. On the other hand, there were exiled writers like Guillermo Cabrera Infante, Reinaldo Arenas, Heberto Padilla and Zoé Valdés who also dabbled with magic realism when they did not focus on the Cuban Revolution, the cause of their exile. In either case, it seemed to me that the substance of my intended book would be diluted rather than enhanced by any attempt at inscribing it within the specificity of nativeness or exile.

A Cuban context that goes beyond History while representing its concrete role lay anchored in the problematics of the look. I consequently thought of a book that drew attention to the breaking of barriers and the restoration of language and vision embedded in T. S. Eliot's metaphor ("a heap of broken images"), not as a self-serving critical prop but as a natural genealogical trope of literary modernism in the Caribbean revolving around Hemingway's role as a cross between Stein, Pound and Eliot in the twenties in Europe, and his demonstrable influence on younger writers in his later years in Cuba.

But for Reinaldo Arenas, Mayra Montero and Abilio Estévez, these younger writers --unlike their elders, Alejo Carpentier, José Lezama Lima, Guillermo Cabrera Infante and Heberto Padilla-- did not extend surrealism, this other feature of Modernism, into their practice of magic realism. Garcia, Walcott, Iyer and Desnoes did the opposite. Their use of minimalism and deconstruction in language pruned of rhetoric clearly brought them in Hemingway's lineage in the Caribbean. As well, Eliot's metaphor and his use of the Waste Land motif were echoed in the function played by Cuban history in their works, and Greene's, in the form of a subtextual process of redefinition.

I identified that process as the bedrock of selected writings by native-born Cubans (Garcia, Desnoes) and temporary residents of Cuba (Hemingway, Walcott, Greene, Iyer). I perceived their works --all of which written or re-written in English-- to stem from a conscious choice to reject impediments to modernity based on nativism, including language. I became intrigued by the fact that their representation of Cuba upped the ante for objectivity in the sense meant by T. S. Eliot's use of the "objective correlative":

The only way of expressing emotion in the form of art is by finding an "objective correlative," in other words, a set of objects, a situation, a chain of events which shall be the formula of that particular emotion; such that when the external facts, which must terminate in sensory experience, are given, the emotion is immediately evoked.(*The Sacred Wood* 100)

There emerged a critical premise worth investigating: a different light was shed on the modern Cuban experience in works related to Euro-American modernism that resorted to innovation in search of catharsis, in a fashion similar to their source in the late nineteenth and early twentieth century.

* * *

This book is conceived as a contribution to literary and cultural history not exclusive of travel and memoir writing, when the writer puts himself or herself on the line. It is grounded in the fact of expatriation, or the status of the writer-as-outsider, behind the origins of Cuban writing in the works of writers like Cirilo Villaverde and José Martí. Their images, fragmented by displacement, are now prolonged in modernist form, as seen in Pico Iyer's homage to Martí in *Cuba and the Night*. I also see this book as a contribution to a literary continuum that transcends barriers, while it indicates how these barriers have impeded the freedom of expression of writers like Reinaldo Arenas whose dying words were more than an ordinary testament:

> I end my life voluntarily because I cannot continue working. Persons near me are in no way responsible for my decision. There is only one person I hold accountable: Fidel Castro. The sufferings of exile, the pain of being banished from my country, the loneliness, and the diseases contracted in exile would probably never have happened if I had been able to enjoy freedom in my country. (*Before Night Falls* 317)

The decision to distance myself from native or exilic positioning paralleled my literary subjects' own distancing in light of the evidence of works censored in Cuba (e.g. Arenas's *Farewell to the Sea*, *The Color of Summer*; Padilla's *Heroes are Grazing in my Garden*, to name a few), and the ones allowed publication since the Revolution that are, but for some few exceptions --like Lezama Lima's *Paradiso* or Desnoes's *Inconsolable Memories*-- tainted with didacticism in the service of the State, or kowtowing to ideological certitudes. This is an admittedly severe judgment, but one based on the adulatory works of the Haitian expatriate writer René Depestre that still earned him the wrath of the regime, Nicolas Guillén's role as the head of Union of Cuban Writers and Artists at the time of the Padilla and Arenas affairs, and what I personally deduced from the list of publications marketed at the State-run Book Fair in early 2003 compared with the official policy of the State towards writing which has apparently remained unchanged since 1971 [See appendix B].

One example will suffice. The American writer Russell Banks was an invited guest at the Book Fair for the launch of the Havana publication of the Spanish translation of his novel, *Affliction*. I was puzzled by the choice of *Affliction*, a psychological novel about a dysfunctional family set in the Northeast of the United States. I could not understand the rationale for choosing *Affliction* over Banks's other novel, *Continental Drift*, a much more contemporary and provocative work in a Caribbean context, until I recalled that its subject was the flight of Haitian boat people to the U.S. That story was obviously too close for comfort in light of Elián Gonzalez's and many more --less lucky-- Cubans' stories of flight at sea. The State publisher chose not to put *Continental Drift* into the "wrong hands."

However, next to Lezama Lima's *Paradiso* which takes place during the pre-revolutionary years, there is the notable exception of Edmundo Desnoes's *Inconsolable Memories*, published in Havana in 1965, revised and translated into English by the author for publication in the U.S. in 1967. Set in Havana in the early days of the Revolution, its subject --the internalization of the problems faced by an artist figure living in the shadow of History-- culminated with the missile crisis of 1962. It is not a desperate need for balance that is reached for by including Desnoes's novel in my selection. As a modernist challenge to barriers, it naturally calls attention to itself when the original Cuban and later American version of the book are compared, and when the addition of the long Hemingway sequence in the latter version acts as a synecdoche. Written by a native Cuban and naturalized American, Desnoes's novel undoubtedly raises essential questions about the maintenance of a space for art and reflection in the crowded arena of Cuba's history.

* * *

The organization of this book around visual and verbal forms is my adaptation of Benitez-Rojo's concept of *carnaval*, when nothing is fixed and everything is flux. As mirrored acts of representation, the visual and the verbal yield a common language based on the image defined by Henri Cartier-Bresson and Ezra Pound as "an intellectual and emotional complex in an instant of time" (*Gardier-Brzeska* 86). The centrality of the image is not denied but enhanced by T. S. Eliot's meditation on the barrenness left when it is broken. The insights of these Imagists corroborate the thinking of Conrad, Sartre and Merleau-Ponty. Applying their related perspectives on the look to the writings of Cristina Garcia, Ernest Hemingway, Derek Walcott, Pico Iyer, Graham Greene, and Edmundo Desnoes, I found a rich field for discussion that deepened the issue of identity and culture whose apparent fragmented, heteroglossic and carnivalesque form in Cuba is merely the tip of an iceberg.

Seen from the perspective of "delayed decoding," this book suggests in the end that the phenomenological, photographic and literary images of Cuba cumulate in meaning not only that there is more than meets the eye, but that what lies unseen is a truth that each onlooker is called upon to discover and ponder.

Preface

by

George Lang

Department of Modern Languages and Cultural Studies

University of Alberta, Edmonton

I trust, Dear Reader, that you will do as I did: leap over the Foreword (and now this Preface too) right to the meat of the text, the Introduction in which Max Dorsinville puts us *in media res*: the "visceral" and existential experience in Cuba which was its culmination and is its frame. Afterwards, you can browse back to the author's Foreword in which the scholarly dimensions of this book are exposed, and even back to this Preface, if you wish.

Welcome back (to those of you who have returned)! As you know, you have in your hands a rather unclassifiable book, one composed in nearly equal parts of autobiography, literary criticism, travelogue, and a gallery of photographs, as well as three appendices, themselves dissimilar: a study of Quebec nationalist culture in the context of concepts which also influenced the Cuban revolution; painfully, the 1971 Cuban doctrine of the purpose of art, still official; and an appreciation of the book from a Haitian perspective.

There is a logic to this heterogeneity, one not unlike the hidden order in chaos about which the exiled Cuban António Benítez-Rojo has written. Benítez-Rojo is in fact one of the critical reference points in *Understanding Contemporary Cuba in Visual and Forms*, and his metaphor of the "repeating island" – the manifold forms of eerily similar although utterly distinct phenomena across the breadth of the Caribbean – surely applies to Max Dorsinville's journey to Cuba. His intellectual, critical and artistic trajectory was not literally a *retour au pays natal* – per Aimé Césaire's *Notebook of a Return to a Native Land*. Dorsinville is

Haitian-born and has lived most of his life in Montréal. But even in the throes of its present tourist-dollar driven "pact with the devil" (he is quoting Fidel Castro here), Cuba remains one of the *repeated* Caribbean islands, a fact the author acknowledges implicitly by dwelling in one chapter on the work of Derek Walcott, whose creative landscape is centered on his own St. Lucia. That a Haitian discovers his own Ellen/ Elena/ Helen in Cuba much as Walcott had configured her in St. Lucia bears testament to the continuity spanning these islands.

To mention Benítez-Rojo is almost automatically to place oneself in a postmodernist perspective. In fact, Dorsinville has deliberately chosen to engage with the modernist canon, largely though not exclusively the Anglo-American one (Hemingway, Graham Greene, Walcott, Pico Iyer, but also Edmundo Desnoes and Cristina Garcia). For critical perspective he turns to Eliot and Pound, and to the mid-century writing in French of Sartre and Merleau-Ponty. Even the visual art Dorsinville has embraced as his own, old-fashioned photography (captured on a Canon pocket "Sure Shot 85 Zoom"), seems out of joint in these times of digital images, camcorders and what-not. "I am not Cartier-Bresson," he writes, but Henri Cartier-Bresson "was my model," in no small part because the French photographer repeatedly captured magic moments of "ordinariness." It is in the flow of ordinariness that the kind of gaze Dorsinville feels to permeate Cuban life can best be caught in images, "merging sight with activities that were communal and inclusive of the gazer and the gazed." Although he does not say so, this modernist perspective makes excellent sense when dealing with a nation whose fleet of cars has survived from a by-gone (modernist) era, and whose public discourse, for reasons there is no need to enumerate here, has remained frozen in time, sealed off by forces both from within and without.

Max Dorsinville's use of Merleau-Ponty contains a hidden irony, since phenomenology aimed at drawing attention to the surface of things and to the ways in which we perceive those surfaces. One aspect of Cuba the author found attractive was an apparent suppression of racism, *par excellence* an ideology of surface and gaze. Yet the constant presence of a seeing and judging Other is a feature both of racism itself and of Cuban culture as Dorsinville construes it, a realm of multiple interpretations, ambiguous intentions, and constantly measured words. Cuba was thus an ideal site in which the acutely-tuned perceptive apparatus of someone himself long subject to racist gaze could express how subtle gazes can and must be interpreted. I refer the reader once again to the Introduction, though this degree of "decoding," as he calls it, is present throughout the text.

Do the disparate pieces of this mosaic hold together? That is something for each reader to decide. Each of us gaze, as we are gazed at. But I would argue that the very Caribbean conclusion to which we are brought on the last page takes it one step beyond the modernist perspective it reclaims. At the beginning of this book we are reminded of T. S. Eliot's condemnation of Western civilization as a "heap of broken images." In conclusion Max Dorsinville, borrowing the words of Derek Walcott, asserts to us that when we "break a vase," the "love that reassembles the fragments is stronger than that love which took its symmetry for granted when it was whole."

Acknowledgments

I have benefited from conversations with a number of individuals in Cuba and outside, most of whom, out of respect for their privacy, are identified under pseudonyms. My wife was extremely supportive throughout our Cuban sojourn. But for her company, I might have missed our flight back to Canada due to a customs officer's conviction that I was a Cuban trying to leave the island undercover. For that kind of support and others, I am naturally grateful.

I appreciate the contribution of several colleagues and former students to the making of this book: Amber for patiently responding to all my inquiries; Lana for her eloquent empathy with the land; Lukas, Allan, Dorothy, Peter and so many others, for kindly lending an ear to my accounting of people and events that are represented in this book. To Charles, a belated acquaintance from Martinique, who told me that he, too, had been mistaken for an illegal Cuban at a Varadero resort, thanks for the shared cathartic laughter.

My gratitude to Professor George Lang, Department of Modern Languages and Cultural Studies, University of Alberta, for his magisterial and stunningly perceptive Preface. I cannot praise enough my colleague Marie-Hélène Laforest, Department of Western Languages, Istituto Universitario Orientale of Naples, for her original contribution to this book. I am also indebted to my colleagues Kathleen Balutansky, Department of English, Saint Michael's College, Maximilien Laroche, Department of Literatures, Université Laval, and Georges Anglade, Department of Geography at Université du Québec à Montréal, for their insightful and informative comments as outside readers.

Last and foremost, my thinking about this book spawned from real-life experiences that included the friendship of Gracia --who asked for *El Galante* whenever she did not see him-- Isabella, for the look in her eyes when she remembered her youthful dancing to Beny Moré's music; Rulfo, the perfect host in his native city, Santa Clara; and Sixto, an enlightened and protective guide. They were the Cuban people at their best: friendly, dignified and graceful.

Introduction

I spent a month in early 2003 in Havana with short stays in Santa Clara and Matanzas. On sabbatical leave from McGill University, I had just completed a massive two-volume collection of postcolonial literary criticism in Africa by the Haitian writer Roger Dorsinville. I was looking for relief from the time-consuming archival research gathering hard-to-find material in Montreal, Port-au-Prince, New York and Paris.

A celebration of the Cuban Revolution for having granted Cuban citizenship to 500,000 Haitian cane cutters in 1959 stood out in a Roger Dorsinville book review I read. It stuck in my mind because he had dramatized that event in one of his novels (*Mourir pour Haïti*, 1975) I edited and translated:

Then there was a thunderous breakthrough: with the stroke of a pen Castro made five hundred thousand *"malditos Haitianos"* into Cubans overnight; no fuss, no questions asked. He just did it.... Have you ever given thought to Castro's miracle, giving a homeland and a future all at once to five hundred thousand of yours?... Five hundred thousand in one sweep, as if some naked and shivering beggars were provided with room and board all at once....Had I been in Cuba in 1959, I'd be a respected citizen by now; I'll never forget that. And don't you ever forget that either...whenever you hear bad things said about Castro or when you're asked to badmouth him in your teaching ("The Mad King," in *The Rule of François ["Papa Doc"] Duvalier* 37-38).

I was reminded of my birthplace, Haiti, which I left in 1954 as a child and visited twenty-nine years later as an adult, and subsequently revisited up to 1991 when chaotic social unrest made it impossible to continue. I was also reminded of my affection for Cuba since my boarding school days in Montreal. I found the right words for that affection when I read Celia del Pino's story in Cristina Garcia's *Dreaming in Cuban* and called it "the romance of the Revolution."

Now that I had completed the fifth and sixth critical edition of Roger Dorsinville's works, I was seized with an urge to travel to Cuba, to effect a journey which neither my uncle nor I had ever made. I knew it was a way for me to celebrate closure, as well as a rite of passage of a sort by turning from the printed page to a hands-on experience with a land and a people I knew from afar, mainly from reading and teaching Caribbean literature.

* * *

Cuba was, in Ian Watt's language, a cumulative "sense impression" tied to "delayed decoding," this "much slower reflexive process of making out [...] meaning" (*Conrad in the Nineteenth Century* 175) behind what would become *Understanding Contemporary Cuba in Visual and Verbal Forms*. From the outset, the word "carnival" obsessively ran in my mind; and Benítez-Rojo's phrase "in 'this certain kind of way'" (borrowed from Sara Gomez's 1974 film, *De Cierta Manera*) summed it up: "In 'this certain kind of way' there is expressed the mystic or magical (if you like) loam of the civilizations that contributed to the formation of Caribbean culture... it takes away the space that separates the onlooker from the participant" (*The Repeating Island* 11-16).

For me, Cuba was Sixto, Rulfo, Maria, Ibis, Gracia, Isabella, and Elena, and all the nameless ones who are in one way or another present in this book: the numerous kids in school uniform in Havana, Santa Clara and Matanzas, the musicians in pick-up bands, the lineups at foodstalls, the domino players and countless *Habaneros* who made the streets of the city "a moveable feast." Cuba, to be sure, was also the constant reminder of History now visited with consumerism (tourism) as I kept seeing the haunting figure of Ché Guevara in Havana, Santa Clara, Matanzas --in fact everywhere, on billboards, buildings, postcards and T-shirts.

The group of students at the University of Havana who spontaneously responded to my request for a photo when I told them I was a visitor from McGill University deserve special mention. Like the young couple I photographed frolicking in the sea of the Bay of Matanzas, they reflected a fluid interracial mix that I like to think makes modern Cuban society unique. Never in our travels in North America, the Caribbean, Europe and Africa did my French-speaking Canadian wife and I feel so at ease in a society where the appearance of diversity was a given, and not a problem.

The fact of diversity (and not the rhetoric of "multiculturalism") greeted us the very first day we landed in Havana. The pictures I took throughout our monthly stay casually recorded it. But it is the intangible quality of "this certain kind of way" that physically and psychologically made me feel at home that I tried to capture in all those Cuban faces. In concrete terms, I saw and befriended ordinary individuals carrying on with their lives in the shadow of History. Their fusion of dignity and resiliency is a spirit that I believe was magnificently represented by the Cuban national I came to know best: Sixto, a third-generation Cuban-Haitian originally from Camagüey.

I met Sixto by chance in Old Havana as I stepped out of a bakery and exclaimed in Creole to my wife that the bread was really hot from the oven. I heard someone respond to me in kind, and I turned and saw a fortyish-looking man on a bike with his son. Time stopped on Avenida Belgica as we chatted in the language of his cane-cutting grandfather who migrated to Cuba from Haiti, and the language I never lost since I left Haiti for Canada. We eagerly exchanged addresses and, acting on his invitation, my wife and I visited him and his family the next day. He returned that visit the day before we flew back to Montreal.

* * *

Roger Dorsinville, I am sure, would have felt gratified by my encounter with Sixto. He was one of those Haitian migrants Castro had transformed into "respected" Cuban citizens proud of their identity. Yet, as he told me, he was a poor man, a former conscript in the Cuban army who had been discharged after sustaining a disabling injury. Since then he worked at two jobs: as a porter at the Havana train station and night watchman in a factory. In either case, his salary was measly. His wife, Maria, a good ten years younger than he, worked in a pharmaceutical plant. His younger son Eliel had not started school and was looked after in a state-run daycare; his oldest son Reydel was in high school.

I visited Sixto and his family in their ramshackle flat at the tail end of a backyard, on the ground floor of a tenement building they shared with two other families. In their dilapidated home, there nonetheless was a big television set, a fridge, a gas stove, an electric fan and a telephone in working order. More importantly, I saw the evidence of a shared sense of community with his neighbors which I mentioned in reply to Sixto's comment about being poor: "You are not poor when you have the richness of family and friends around you."

Both on that day and when he came to say goodbye, we talked extensively. I learned a lot about his daily life as an ordinary worker whose dismal apartment was just a stone's throw away from the tourist attractions of Old Havana. He said he had never set foot in any of the restaurants and hotels whose fares I described to him. He told me about the limitations of food rationing (pointing to his youngest son, he said he did not know what beef tasted like); but he also talked about the benefits of free health care and education. He, like others, grumbled at the omnipresent bureaucracy, but he informed me that the Committees for the Defense of the Revolution on every street did not mean enforced attendance at their monthly meetings. He never said a bad word about the regime, and, like others, references to names, events tied to the Revolution were cautiously worded *sotto voce*.

In answer to a query about color prejudice, he asked me to repeat my question. He apparently did not understand what I was talking about. When he did understand, his point was that the Revolution had eradicated racism and replaced it with a sense of national identity that made all Cubans one and the same. I refrained from telling him that I noticed the predominance of fair-skinned Cubans in all fields; i.e. the political, intellectual, scientific and educational leadership. I did not point out that on the three state-run television channels I saw just one Bryant Gumbel-like Cuban co-hosting a clone of NBC's *Today* morning show called *Buenos Dias* ("Good Morning"), or that I had seen just one single Afro-Cuban teacher on the numerous televised courses. (In contrast, I saw a lot of Afro-Cubans on variety shows and sportscasts....)

I let my doubts rest when I witnessed the behavior of the owner of the *casa particular* where I was staying the day Sixto came for a visit. Neither Isabella (a fair-skinned Cuban), her cleaning lady, Gracia (a *mestizo*), nor Sixto displayed any apparent sense of inhibition or unease. My wife, on the other hand, later told me in Montreal that she thought they showed a rather eager interest in asking about the circumstances of our meeting with Sixto. (Just as on the day I went to Matanzas and she stayed in Havana she could not understand why the two ladies appeared to be so shocked.)

At any rate, for someone used to the revealing ritualized signs characteristic of interracial interaction (or lack of) in North America, I carefully tried to detect the manifestation of some kind of self-consciousness in either one of my Cuban friends. Throughout that morning on the terrace of the *casa particular*, as Gracia and Isabella moved about, casually joining in my exchanges with Sixto, even enlarging our circle by chatting with neighbors whose windows opened on the terrace, I failed to see any evidence of "tap dancing." (A metaphor borrowed from Muhammad Ali. I never forgot how he derisively shuffled his feet by way of answering an interviewer's question about his refusal to fight in Vietnam.) It meant subaltern behavior. That morning, Sixto looked like anything but a subaltern. He, Gracia and Isabella showed no sign other than that they were Cubans talking to each other as equals.

In a society controlled by rigid patterns of conditioned behavior for more than forty years of the Revolution, I wondered whether my friends were not instinctively acting out a politically-correct line for my benefit as a foreigner. I knew that the official line on racial prejudice was spelled out, most recently in February 2003, by Fidel Castro in a televised speech at an international conference on education in Havana. Racism, said Castro, was a generic blight on world history and, more specifically, on pre-revolutionary Cuba that the Revolution was committed to eradicating by way of education and the carrying out of the teachings of José Martí (its intellectual father revered as "the apostle" whose statue is not only at the center of the Plaza de la Revolución in Havana but on practically every street corner of the island) on the multiracial nature of Cuban society.

After all, I had noticed how certain subjects were addressed indirectly, if at all, when a show of misunderstanding due to language was set aside; or how voices were lowered and sideway glances preceded any guarded reference to the government. (The name of El Comandante Jefé, for instance, was never uttered. A question about his oldest son, Fidelito, whose pictures I recall seeing in the early days of the Revolution, brought the cryptic answer that he was an engineer. Nothing more.)

* * *

Since leaving Cuba, I have wondered at times about my rather extraordinary chance meeting with Sixto. (Cubans of Haitian ancestry are more likely to be found in the eastern region of Cuba where their forebears migrated to work in the sugar cane plantations.) Was my meeting with a former soldier on the street all that serendipitous in a society I came to know where everyone's behavior was a constant amendment of overt obedience to the official line? Mulling over the extent of government control on individual lives and, by inference, the likelihood of more than casual scrutiny of visitors like me who did not follow the standard route of the all-inclusive, out-of-the-way resorts, I more than wondered about the implications of my sharing a surname with Roger Dorsinville who was known to the Cuban authorities as far back as 1961 when, as a member of the Haitian delegation at a conference in Costa Rica of the Organization of American States, he voted against the ostracization of the Castro regime: "The reaction of the American delegation led by secretary Dillon, when faced by our insistence to save Castro, can only be compared to the Cubans' own surprise. Led by Raúl Roa, they came over to thank and congratulate us, promising us any form of collaboration" (*Memoirs of Haiti* 176).

Or was his name perhaps known in connection with *Mourir pour Haïti*, the novel mentioned earlier, when he gave high praise to Castro?

I may have been indulging in speculations and wishful thinking; but no more and no less than the society that at times claimed me as much as I came to claim it as part of myself. I was indulging in the diffidence and covert tactics in everyday discourse I witnessed. In real terms, "this certain kind of way" meant the survival tactics a long-suffering people instinctively resorted to throughout its history (something known as "marronnage" in my native land, and "outfoxing the Massa," in the American south). How else account for the number of times ordinary individuals pretended ignorance when I asked for simple directions during my stay or on my way out to the airport when I pointed to what looked like water reservoirs jutting out in the landscape and the taxi driver pretended he did not know what they were?

I became wise to the everyday use of subterfuge when I overheard a neighbor who pretended he did not speak English fluently give directions (with an American accent!) to some tourists. It was the same everyday pretense that the licensed cab drivers resorted to, negotiating fares dispensing them from filling out forms forcing them to turn in their earnings to the government. Wasn't covert individual behavior, then, a logical subversive reaction to official behavior such as the State-run bus companies' when they sold one-way and not return tickets, or when they did not supply bus schedules?

I knew from experience in Matanzas of a ticket seller's annoyance at my requesting a return ticket to Havana and her insistence that I simply show up on time when the bus stopped on its way back from Varadero. I was left to ponder the possibility of the bus being full and having to fend for myself on how to spend the night in Matanzas, hoping for the best the next day.... There seemed to be a connection between another ticket seller's congeniality at the Havana bus terminal on another occasion --smilingly telling me, "you look Cuban," as she promised she would see to my lodging in Santa Clara with her friend Teresita-- and her smiling wordlessness when, returning from Santa Clara, I stopped by to let her know everything turned out fine. There were other people around; she merely smiled and nodded, letting me guess whether she understood what I was talking about.

My experience of the Cubans' multifaceted behavior lay behind my musings about the existence of some connection between sharing a surname with a former Haitian diplomat and writer, a third-generation Cuban-Haitian retired soldier and my feeling so welcome in Cuba. Or was the fact of my being a first-generation Haitian-Canadian simply blurred with fiction when I was mistaken for a Cuban, as I later found out?

Fact and fiction, I discovered, were hardly distinct in Cuba. "This certain kind of way" was interwoven with "looking Cuban," when I compared my going through customs on arrival and departure at the José Martí International Airport, one month later. The apparently innocuous question asked by an Afro-Cuban woman as I looked for my luggage after landing --"Where are you from?"-- should have alerted me to the implications of what she left unsaid but was frequently voiced later on: "You look Cuban." I took *parece Cubano* to be a simple, gracious remark meant to make me feel welcome. But what to me was a metaphorical expression meant something else for a suspicious-looking customs officer on my way out of the country.

* * *

My interpretation of the interaction at the *casa particular* between Sixto, Gracia and Isabella the morning before I left Cuba confirmed, either as genuine fact or as conditioned behavior resulting in fiction, what seemed to be a lasting achievement of the Cuban Revolution. The issue of race had apparently been displaced if not erased in Cuba. Jean-Paul Sartre's famous pronouncement in *Orphée noir* (1948) --"Negritude...aims at preparing the synthesis or realization of the human being in a raceless society" (*Black Orpheus* 447)-- seemed to have come to fruition.

As fact or fiction, revolutionary Cuba spawned, I thought, a society where the notion of race or skin color was replaced, for better or for worse, with a sense of national identity that took the diversity of racial extraction as a given, and not a problem. In that light, my typical Canadian adherence to invisibility as a code for tolerance in a multicultural society was due for reassessment. Under the Cuban look, my skin color was a fact associated with Cubans only in a society that seldom saw foreign Blacks. The best-known were African-Americans --evidenced by the number of Michael Jordan and Michael Jackson T-shirts I saw in Havana, for instance-- but American blacks were at a mythical distance, unlikely to visit Cuba due to the U.S. embargo. African-Canadians were simply not known to exist, as a young Afro-Cuban told me in Santa Clara. As for genuine Africans, they were known as the remote cousins the Revolution had rediscovered and fought for in Angola and Ethiopia; but they were not seen in Cuba. Black West Indians, on the other hand, had long ago been nationalized as "Cubans," witness Sixto.

Thus, what to me was fiction when I was told now and then that I looked Cuban was a fact for the customs officer. Too bewildered to understand right away why he wanted *"un otro documento"* (another document) --after I showed him my Canadian passport-- and tempted to read stupidity on his face when he asked me where I was born ("Haiti!... It says so right there on the passport," I silently said to myself), I was puzzled.

I recalled I had *"un otro documento"* and showed him my citizenship card with my picture going back to 1972 with a full Afro hairdo and void of the mustache I have been wearing since. I chuckled inside wondering whether he would tell me next that the picture did not look like me. He hardly glanced at it. Then he asked the reason for my stay in Cuba. I replied, "vacation," but I could tell his mind was elsewhere. He went on: "Are you traveling alone?" I said I was with my wife and pointed to her being next in line outside the cubicle. He could not see her. That last piece of information seemed to provide him with an outlet. He gave me a final look. I noticed his beribboned uniform, tinted glasses and lined, middle-aged face. He was a career military man, not just an ordinary customs officer. The frown that never left his face meant he had been dead serious all along. Then he mumbled the equivalent of "OK" and waived me off.

My wife later told me she heard everything and braced herself to "let him have it" when the officer's first question to her was to confirm whether we were married. She replied, "Yes," and stressed every one of the next syllables, "for thirty-nine years!" He grimaced a smile. No more questions.

To the obviousness of the officer's unspoken assumption that I was a Cuban using a Canadian passport to make his way out of Cuba should be added, equally obviously, "this certain kind of way." His smile reflected his adding two and two together. That fellow was Cuban, he thought, but he had a wife who did not look Cuban. And he carried a *bona fide* Canadian passport. That was up his alley: the stuff of fiction, magic realism! His grimaced smile to my wife meant he got the joke.... Someone else's turn now.

* * *

Fact and fiction became more entwined on the flight back., when "someone else's turn" came up. The plane was smaller than the one mentioned at the Cubana Airlines' reservation desk. There were three seats on each side of a narrow aisle. Our seats were not in what my wife thought would be the first-class section. They were up front, all right, but one row short of first-class from which we were separated by a partition. We were to stare at this blank wall, between looking outside the window (I had the window seat) and at an insipid movie on a minute screen overhead.

The plane was practically full and the door was about to close. Two loud Spanish-speaking men then came on board, a middle-aged fat one in an open-necked shirt with grizzled gray hair on his protruding chest, and a tall, thirtyish, athletic-looking one. The middle-aged man sat in the aisle seat behind his friend after wrangling with a French-Canadian passenger whose carry-on luggage he unceremoniously removed from the overhead bin to make room for his own. His gravelly voice carried loud and with finality as he dismissed the passenger's objections ("Did you buy this plane?") by calling on a flight attendant's support for his right to replace the man's luggage with his own. He switched to English during the flight, badgering a young South American woman behind me because she would not speak to him in Spanish. I heard her reply she preferred to speak French now that she lived in Quebec. My wife and I noticed he patted her behind when she slid by his seat on her way to the bathroom.

But it was his friend, the thirtyish-looking one, that I observed at close range (just as he, too, observed me while pretending not to). He sat in our row, in the aisle seat next to my wife whom he courteously greeted. Throughout the flight he initiated small talk with her ranging from asking whether she was French to an odd display of impatience when we were approaching Montreal. My wife's reply to his mention of snow on the ground ("It's icy") for some reason seemed to annoy him ("No, I didn't say icy!"). He never said a word to me, not even when I said the lights on the ground were Montreal's. I had included him in my remark, looking at him. He averted his eyes, and verbal non-contact was kept.

He kibbitzed with the flight attendants, though. I thought they were either taken in by his good looks or knew him, or both. At mealtime, my wife noticed he was served two dinners. He crossed his legs; he had clogs on, the kind casually worn in the city in the summer by the hip crowd, but not at the beach --be it Varadero where his tanned look pretended he stayed. His choice of footwear struck me as odd for someone about to land in winter in Montreal. Moreover, he was not wearing socks. Later on, I thought that this fact and the clogs may have been the reason for his concern about snow on the ground. His impatient reply to my wife was maybe due to his rude awakening to the realization that winter in Montreal meant snow or ice --at any rate, cold weather-- a fact that seemingly eluded his comprehension.

I overheard his chatting up one of the flight attendants on her schedule for the evening. When she replied the crew was set to return the same night to Havana he said that he,too,would be on the flight. As we were standing in line waiting for the plane door to open, I caught his gazing at my wife when she walked by. He had put on a black, military-like beret. Standing in front of me, I guessed he was at least six-foot tall, with a trained physique that was neither that of a bodybuilder nor the prissy one of a Latin American ladies' man, the image he had worked hard to get across.

He had obviously put on an act during the flight, expecting me to fall for the bait. At his age, I told off guys like him too eager to prove something to themselves. I was older now and better acquainted with mind games when it came to "upmanship." And I was fresh out of an intensive one-month seminar on sub-textual discourse in Cuba, in light of which his inquisitive company may have been the final exam. So, I wisely chose to wait and see. I waited and nothing happened. The last I saw of him was his standing in line, waiting for the plane door to open.

I did not see him going through Canadian customs, nor did I see him waiting for his luggage. The hefty black duffel bag he carried on board was apparently all that he had. What lay behind his acting?

What lay behind the Cuban flight attendants' cold glances at the one black guy on the plane (*me*, the *parece Cubano* one who was fleeing the island undercover with a white companion!) that did not escape my notice while they went about with their knee bends and bunny hops with our travel companion? My wife was spared (she asked for chicken) but I am of the opinion that the chewy, greyish beef plate one of the attendants coldly dropped on my lap was a parting gift from whomever was "someone else." Starting the day after my return to Montreal I was reminded for one week of that "parting gift" with a severe case of gastroenteritis. During repeated runs to the bathroom, I feverishly and nauseously recalled Sixto's line about his son not knowing what beef tasted like. How lucky of him, I thought, if it meant what I had been served....

* * *

My eyes were opened by chance or design as a result of my encounter with Sixto, and the guidance he provided. As mentioned earlier, I learned to decode subtexts in what otherwise seemed innocent. Was the customs officer's suspicion a natural outgrowth of the Cuban sense of national identity? Was I privy to a revealing insight on the extent of control exercised by the State over its citizens in the matter of (the nonexistent) freedom to travel? Did I witness an intriguing display of miscommunication between the instances that let us in --after verification presumably even before we boarded Cubana Airlines in Montreal on our way in-- and those that were to let us out?

And who were those "instances" who apparently did not interfere with us during our one-month stay, except for the mysterious disappearance from a closet in our apartment of some newspapers we meant to take back to Montreal? Though I am not naive enough to think that we were not monitored as early as when we made reservations on the Internet for the *casa particular*, my wife --who tends to see the bright side of things and turn a blind eye to their opposite-- was the one whose eyes were now wide open to the reality of cloak-and-dagger, Cuban style. Maybe my wife is right: "See no evil, hear no evil...." Not knowing has to be a virtue when the space between the unsuspecting *onlooker* and the *participant* is nullified, resulting in the rich, learning experience that Cuba proved to be.

* * *

Beyond the hands-on carnivalesque run of events that had to be factually told first, the conception and the writing of this book owe a lot to my reading Joseph Conrad, Jean-Paul Sartre, Maurice Merleau-Ponty, Antonio Benítez-Rojo, Cristina Garcia, Ernest Hemingway, Derek Walcott, Graham Greene, Edmundo Desnoes, years before I traveled to Cuba, and my subsequent discovery of the writings of Pico Iyer. My understanding of their works was enhanced in the wake of my stay in Cuba. Once I reconciled myself with the written word, I turned to them for documented support of the kind of narrative I planned to write.

I am particularly indebted to Joseph Conrad whose celebration of literary impressionism was a learned inspiration: "...to make you hear, to make you feel -- it is, before all, to make you *see!*" ("Preface," *The Nigger of the 'Narcissus'* xlix). Although Conrad's medium --"The power of the written word," *Ibid.*-- had wearied me in pursuit of Roger Dorsinville's critical work, I knew that I would return to it after a temporary distancing. And in the process, Conrad's narrative device Ian Watt calls "delayed decoding" (*Ibid.*) became integral to the writing of this book.

Maurice Merleau-Ponty is the other writer who restored for me the adequacy of language for the rendering of experience. I re-read his writings on perception (especially his masterwork, *Phenomenology of Perception*) subsequent to my return from Cuba and found in his thinking a conceptual anchor for what I had looked for and tried to grasp during my stay in Cuba.

There, I relied on my perception of things as they appeared to me in everyday life --what in phenomenology Merleau-Ponty describes as "the gaze [that] gets more or less from things according to the way in which it questions them, ranges over or dwells on them" (*Phenomenology of Perception* 153). I learned to see beyond the omnipresence of History in the spoken words heard on TV, in public ceremonies, the written words daily read in *Granma* and *Rebelde Juventud*. I saw how those "official" words were misleading when they were counterpointed by the ordinary people's own unofficial language.

Theirs was free of rhetoric: it was sarcastic (referring to the "sameness" of public discourse), iconoclastic ("that's old," said in answer to a request for revolutionary marches in a record store), subversive (the gestual of tight jeans and midriff bareness boldly flaunted by twenty-year olds to ensnare naive middle-aged foreigners and secure their only way out of the island by marrying them), gross ("You act like a mulatto," when one resisted the entreaties of entrapment), and always deceptively innocent-like ("When are you coming back?" i.e. "When will you bring back presents and other goodies for me?").

And always, I saw the carnivalesque carousel of daily living where no one remained an *onlooker*. People always *looking* at you, *testing* you: "Being watched is just part of everyday life in Cuba, but I never got used to it," says David Alan Harvey, the co-author of *Cuba* (17).

* * *

Cubans looked at me, and I looked at them. This book tells through their look and mine, in words and pictures, how I became a *participant* in the carousel, and learned as much about myself as I learned about them. In fact, it is hard to separate one from the other; which is precisely what Merleau-Ponty means ("The theory of the body is already a theory of perception,"*Phenomenology of Perception* 203). Nowhere else but in Cuba, perhaps, can one find the validation of such a key idea in Merleau-Ponty's thinking than in the customs officer's look fixed on me rather than on the coded form of closure of a passport. He, of all people, was questioning the official certainties of identity tied to nationality against his own perception of the body he saw in front of him, silently thinking it belonged to him; i.e. his nation or his inculcated idea of the nation based on the look of things.

This narrative is about the elusiveness of perception when the physical, sensorial realm against which perception is tested is as elemental as the silent, omnipresent look unique to Cuba. Indeed, how does one read a silent language? This book, if anything, addresses that central question. As a way of mapping the territory I plan on exploring, a few considerations on what appears to be the uniqueness of the Cuban look are in order.

I suggest that this "uniqueness" is more than the constant state of alert maintained by the government and internalized by its citizens since the advent of the Revolution; a context which for Reinaldo Arenas means that "Informing on others is something most Cubans do every day" (*Before Night Falls* 203) or that a character in Pico Iyer's *Cuba and the Night* nervously characterizes as constant spying ("Everyone is a spy. Everywhere, they are listening," 34). Other than a reiteration of an Orwellian Big Brother watching, a cynically learned survival tactic, or an instance of dehumanization in relationships, the Cuban look has metamorphosed since 1959 into a way of life, a style congruent to perception as spectacle, a ritual shared by gazer and gazed. [Of Indian parentage, Pico Iyer bemusedly reports in *Falling Off the Map*, his travel book, that he, too, was mistaken for a Cuban illegally on the premises of a resort in Varadero, 62.] The fixity of the look is akin to a photo: a deceptive pause or pose, a protective and decorative mask beyond which lies an organic, rhythmic vital pace in the manner Benítez-Rojo associates with *carnaval* (*The Repeating Island* 29).

The Cuban look masks an act of consciousness and remembrance. On a daily basis, and in the openness of the city or the countryside, it ritualizes the preservation of the self constantly measuring itself in the mirror of the other. Such a practice is epistemological and not the reductive consequence of ideology, because ideology over a period of more than forty years of the Revolution has long been internalized and subverted in the daily and omnipresent practice of subterfuge, of which the *look* is emblematic.

A deeper and more haunting truth is the creation in practice of a fertile ground for the maintenance of free communication because the shared look is a communal, albeit silent, language. The *look* explains why modernist theory with its stress on silence, subtext underlying surface appearance, analogizing of truth in the image of the iceberg, or the image unifying emotion and reason, renewed itself in Cuba. As a cultural trope, the Cuban look contains all these features of modernist theory, a correspondence perceived by all the writers in this book who chose to give verbal expression to Cuba's silent language.

Chapter One

The Nature of the Look: Garcia's *Dreaming in Cuban*

Jean-Paul Sartre visited Cuba in the early days of the Revolution. *Sartre on Cuba* (1961) is his factual reportage based on what he saw revolving around Fidel Castro and his youthful comrades. Basically, Sartre eschewed philosophical speculations in favor of accounting for the practice of a revolution which he uncritically admired. No doubt because he saw the Revolution as an existential act unraveling in the process of rapid decision-making he witnessed by traveling around the island with Fidel Castro, and meeting late at night with the apparently sleepless Ché Guevara, he celebrated the youthfulness of the revolutionaries. In addition to the Castro brothers, Ché Guevara, Armando Hart, Antonio Nuñez Jimenez and others appeared to him as existential heroes making choices, creating History "on the run" in the absence of a pre-existing model to chart their course.

Sartre curiously refrained from any criticism of the activism which stood for doctrine, nor did he anticipate questions about the socialist model the revolutionaries were in fact turning to. The single occasion he apparently did, in a lecture at the University of Havana on the relationship between ideology and revolution (with the examples of his own country and the USSR in mind), he quickly retreated from delving into its implications for Cuba (146-160). Altogether, *Sartre on Cuba* is a celebration of the Revolution by an unconditional admirer. Read years after the euphoria of the early days, the book seems to be outdated, a mere period piece, but for the redeeming motif of the gaze of the philosopher seeing as in a mirror the transformed image of Roquentin (the anti-hero of his 1938 novel, *La Nausée*). The picture of Castro or Guevara that Sartre paints is Roquentin changing from nothingness to being, passivity to activism, cerebralness to visceralness. In short, the Cuban revolutionary seemed to be the concrete manifestation of the anti-hero turned into existential hero.

Sartre, indeed, had a predilection for History in the image of the Black, the Jew, or the colonized individual whom he identified as an existential hero whose absence in his own fiction was filled by the reality he saw unfolding in post-World War II. Thus he wrote *Orphée noir*, a Preface for Léopold Sédar Senghor's 1948 anthology of Black writing, followed by his *Réflexions sur la question juive* (1954), and his Preface to Frantz Fanon's *The Wretched of the Earth* (1961). *Sartre on Cuba* was not just a topical reportage but another example of Sartre's shock of recognition when faced with otherness. Cuba was another terrain for the illustration of his ideas harking back to *L'Etre et le néant*.

But Cuba, in contrast to other experiences, was a live occurrence Sartre witnessed firsthand. He saw what an existential hero looked like through the exercise of his own gaze. His encounter with history in the making yielded a perception denied in his fiction. *Sartre on Cuba* was very relevant to the principal concept of *Understanding Contemporary Cuba* --the *look* as self-reflexive-- in addition to subtextually illustrating the idea that self and otherness are one.

* * *

Sartre is the first modern thinker to theorize on the *look*, or the *gaze*. In *L'Etre et le néant* (*Being and Nothingness*, 1943), he argues for the indissociable linkage between individual self-awareness and the presence of the other through the latter's gaze. In *Huis-clos (No Exit)*, his 1944 play, he emblematized the problematical reach for identity when "hell is others." Sartre confronted the individual existentialist stance with the specific historical examples of the marginalization of minorities. In *Reflexions sur la question juive* (*Anti-Semite and Jew*, 1954) he stated that the Jew is the "other's" creation. And he began *Orphée noir* (*Black Orpheus*, 1948) by referring to the impact of modern Black writing as the shock of "otherness" on the sensibility of the reader: "Today, these black men are looking at us, and our gaze comes back to our own eyes..." (in J. Chametzky and S. Kaplan, eds. *Black and White in American Culture* 415).

In one form or another, Sartre consistently drew on the binary of self and otherness as a central paradigm of the modern sensibility locked in self-destructive alienation until such time as the oneness of self and otherness is achieved in awareness, choice and action. In fact, Sartre gave a conceptual anchoring to Joseph Conrad's dramatization of the relatedness of binarism in his 1899 novel, *Heart of Darkness*. Making use of a symbolic journey in an African setting, Conrad portrayed how Marlow's search for Kurtz resulted in the end with the former discovering his double in the latter, his own self-reflection.

Though Sartre refers to a writer like William Faulkner, who obviously learned from Conrad (see especially *Sanctuary* 1931, and *Light in August*, 1932), he makes no mention of Conrad in *Being and Nothingness*. But he does refer to Schopenhauer, Nietzsche and Hegel who were familiar to Conrad (see Ian Watt's *Conrad in the Nineteenth Century*), and shaped his own thinking and Conrad's on the dialectic of doubleness. Hegelian dialectics, in particular, underlies the conclusion of Sartre's *Black Orpheus:* the disappearance of Negritude in a raceless society subsequent to Negritude's antithetic opposition to the thesis of racism. Similarly, Marlow's journey in the Congo closes on a Hegelian note, with a silent Marlow caught "in the pose of a meditating Buddha" (*Heart of Darkness* 121).

Any number of writers across cultures and nations have since Conrad and Sartre voiced the modern consciousness confronting binaries and dichotomies in a search for meaning. The names of Nathanael West, F. Scott Fitzgerald, Richard Wright, Ralph Ellison can be added to William Faulkner in American literature. The works of Chinua Achebe, J.M. Coetzee, Wilson Harris, Michael Ondaatje, and Salman Rushdie readily come to mind in the field of postcolonial literature.

All the more reason to turn to British writer John Berger and his book, *Ways of Seeing*, for a more direct contextualization of binarism leading to my use of a concept like the *look*, or the *gaze*, in a Cuban context. Already, I have suggested how my approach in the making of this book incorporates existential (Sartre), phenomenological (Merleau-Ponty) and cultural philosophy (Benítez-Rojo) tied to a theory of photography (Cartier-Bresson) that mirrors a key tenet of Imagism (Pound). I have argued up to this point for a melding of opposites, the fusion of the *onlooker* and the *participant* making one the gazer and the gazed in a metaphorical carousel. How does my approach stand when confronted with

Berger's understanding of the relationship between the gazer and the gazed from the perspective of gender?

Ways of Seeing has enjoyed wide currency in academic circles (in my own department at McGill I can recall any number of student essays whose arguments rested on gender dichotomization as argued by Berger). Its key arguments are worth re-stating. First, Berger radicalizes the concept of the look when he says that it is predicated on gender affiliation. Second, the look, for him, is reflective of a power relationship between the sexes. Third, the male gazer is seen as the one possessing "power": "A man's presence suggests what he is capable of doing to you or for you" (46). The woman's presence, on the other hand, "...defines what can and cannot be done to her" (*Ibid.*). More significantly, according to Berger, "to be born a woman has been to be born within an allotted and confined space, into the keeping of men" (*Ibid.*). Admittedly, Berger proceeds with an analysis of the evidence supportive of his thesis from the perspective of art history.

Removed from the specifics of art history and widely adopted as part of the contemporary feminist discourse, Berger's thesis has undoubtedly been perceived and espoused (ironically or not) by a duality of perception in readership dependent on the same gender dichotomy that he argues in his thesis. When, in addition, it is considered that Berger's notion of power directly derives from Marx's thinking on the subject we get a broader conceptual anchoring for gender dichotomization. Berger incorporates the duality of the male gazer and the gazed female within the uneven distribution of power between masters and slaves, haves and have-nots, colonizers and colonized, dominant and dominated, posited by dialectical materialism.

Berger's approach represents, then, a resurgence of the kind of binarism that Existentialism, with Sartre and his followers, had apparently deconstructed.

* * *

A response to Berger is found in Cristina Garcia's 1992 novel, *Dreaming in Cuban*, which addresses History, power, perception, gender dichotomization and, of course, the visual arts. Photography, for instance, is positioned as the starting point of the love affair between Celia del Pino and Gustavo Sierra de

Armas (he meets her in a photography shop and he buys a camera from her because "he wanted to document the murders in Spain through a peephole in his overcoat," 35-36). A photo of El Lider is kept by Celia at her bedside: it iconizes her unrequited love for Gustavo she transferred to the mythical figure of El Lider, and it also defines her commitment to the Revolution and the assertion of power it represents, and of which she is part as a people's court judge.

On the other hand, her granddaughter Pilar is an artist whose return to her homeland is associated with her work as a visual artist. She is a painter and in her gaze she sees the predominance of the color blue: "Until I returned to Cuba, I never realized how many blues exist" (233). Her painting is her own relationship with power: through art she sees creation, transformation and control over History. She imagines telling El Lider: "Art, I'd tell him is the ultimate revolution," 235).

Both Celia and Pilar are defined by their gaze. The novel opens with Celia gazing through binoculars from her doorstep, "guarding the north coast of Cuba" (3). Pilar is introduced in the dressing room of a department store as she glimpses her father engaged in a tryst with a woman. She follows them at a distance and her thoughts revolve around the initial shock of seeing her father's behavior ("Shit! I can't believe this!" 25). Her decision to return to Cuba is directly connected with the sighting of her father ("That's it. My mind's made up. I'm going back to Cuba," 25).

Sight, for Pilar, is a rite of passage connecting awareness, choice and action in her quest for self-assertion. Self-reflexively, sight authentifies her control over the narrative as the artist figure who inherits her grandmother's letters, memory and legacy of resiliency and strength. In retrospect, the split, fragmented form of the narrative suggests how a work of art is graphically constructed out of the ruins of History. Celia's closing words referring to Pilar as the one who "will remember everything" (245) emphasize that memory is connected with identity. Her words and her granddaughter's are signs that draw attention to both speakers' relationship with themselves and others through sight: Pilar's as a painter and Celia's in an internalized vision of love, revolution and History iconized by the photograph of El Lider.

The other major female characters in the novel, the two sisters, Lourdes and Felicia (respectively Pilar's mother, and her aunt), as well as Herminia (Felicia's friend), are all defined on the border of marginalization. Lourdes is an immigrant to the U.S.; Felicia is a dysfunctional, abused woman; and Herminia is the daughter of a disenfranchised *Santeria* priest. They seem to embody John Berger's categorization of the figure of the woman things-are-being-done-to, but for the fact that each one is defined less by her social identification than by strengths located in her clearsighted, though disguised, sense of self.

Lourdes' gaze, for example, is deceptively covered up by her looking like the stereotypical immigrant fed on the American Dream (her bakery is called "Yankee Doodle," 142). The hidden power of her sight is an echo of her mother's quixotic gazing. Both stand on guard on different shores they mean to protect. Lourdes' sight further matches her mother's in connection with her reading Pilar's diary that incorporates the tales of remembrance told in the letters passed on to Pilar by Celia.

Felicia's empowerment is like her mother's, relying on vision she tells her son, Ivanito: "Imagination, like memory, can transform lies to truths" (88). She urges him, "You must imagine winter, Ivanito" (*Ibid.*), for survival. As she dances with him to Beny Moré's "I am what I am" she also metaphorically articulates a physical relationship with the world based on harmony: "Everything makes sense when they dance" (78). (Her mother's dream of dancing the flamenco in Spain and meeting again with Gustavo is, of course, her own way of "making sense" of everything.)

Herminia, on the other hand, gets to tell the story of Felicia from the marginalized perspective of a dark-skinned Cuban and the practice of *Santeria*. She says: "There is something else, something very important. Felicia is the only person I've known who didn't see color.... I trust only what I see..." (184-185). What she sees in Felicia is a twin-like figure who is doubled, like her, by social strictures. Both transcend those strictures by relying on clearsightedness, a controlling belief in themselves and not the State or a male-dominated society.

Felicia's three failed marriages symbolized by the destructiveness of fire (Hugo's disfigurement, Ernesto's death in a kitchen fire, and Otto's by electrocution) personalize the conflictual relationship with the male figure of power identified by Herminia: "One thing hasn't changed: the men are still in charge. Fixing that is going to take a lot longer than twenty years" (185).

Herminia's words are ironic in the overall context of the narrative which, among so many patterns of deconstruction, consistently represents the male figure of power not as someone "whose presence can do things to you," in Berger's formulation (and, admittedly, demonstrated in Hugo's behavior early in his relationship with Felicia; and the rape and scarification Lourdes is subjected to), but as someone seen in recurrent images of disintegration from a woman's point of view.

Jorge, Celia's husband, is a ghost figure sighted on the Cuban shore by Celia. He is the same ghost figure who haunts Lourdes in Brooklyn because he holds the key to her failed rapport with her mother. Rufino, Pilar's father, spends his days either pursuing mirage-like blondes or locked in his workshop idly inventing useless contraptions. Hugo, Felicia's first husband, is a grotesque, disfigured monster created out of Felicia's revenge. Javier, Celia's only son, returns from Europe his wife having left him, and he is dying of cancer.

Not a single male figure of significance is spared the iconoclastic gaze embedded in the narrative, but for the exception of Ivanito who is at any rate a child figure who exists as a projection of his mother's dream vision extended by his aunt Lourdes in the end: "We'll go to Disney World this summer" (239).

Altogether, a close analysis of Cristina Garcia's *Dreaming in Cuban*, from the perspective of vision in its many complex forms, leads to the conclusion that her novel reverses John Berger's schematization through art history of the nature, function and significance of the look in a power relationship ruled by men. For Garcia, History has evolved. The male is no longer the instrument of intimidating power (for instance, when El Lider is seen at the end of the book, he is described as looking old, "smaller, too, more vulnerable, a caricature of himself," 236), nor is the woman the passive figure to-whom-things-are-done. It is as if Cristina Garcia were perfectly cognizant of John Berger's categories (which is not improbable given the publication date of Berger's book, 1972; moreover, given the character of Pilar as a student who spent one semester studying art history in Venice). Her awareness seems to extend to one of Berger's sources on the relationship between perceptual consciousness and the body. Merleau-Ponty's "the subject that I am, when taken concretely, is inseparable from this body and the world" (*Phenomenology of Perception* 408) is echoed in Berger's "to be born a woman has been to be born within an allotted and confined space" (76). Fully aware of the conceptualization of the body in modern European thought, Cristina Garcia sets out to deconstruct it largely from her own cultural experience as a Cuban.

However, Garcia's deconstruction of Berger's notion of the gaze also appears to be based on gender, albeit reversing Berger's power relationship. In so doing, her perspective might seem derivative of a feminist aesthetic foregrounding the woman's self-empowerment. Since such an agenda entails the displacement of the masculine voice or point of view (including Berger's, as sympathetically received as it was initially by feminists), the old binarism of self and otherness is given a new formulation. The "othered" woman of Berger is now replaced by Garcia's "othered" man.

Yet, Garcia's apparent feminist discourse is tempered by the gaze as metaphor in a Cuban context. Antonio Benítez-Rojo describes a threshold point during the missile crisis of 1962 that he personally witnessed. He uses striking imagery to describe his sighting of two old black women beneath his balcony on the day that Cuba, if not the world, was faced with annihilation. He dwells on their way of walking, scent, gesture, chatter, and concludes: "I knew then at once that there would be no apocalypse" (*Ibid*.10). Answering his own unspoken question ("Why?"), he argues that apocalyptic finality is a notion foreign to Cuban culture; that in the face of death or other ominous occurrence the characteristic rejoinder is "Here I am fucked, but happy" (10).

Benítez-Rojo's reference to an existential stance borne by the image of the two women at a precise point in history suggests that the essence of Cuban culture --shared by Cristina Garcia-- is not gender bound or reducible to the gender categorization argued by Berger. Neither Benítez-Rojo's nor Garcia's gaze is locked on imbalance in gender representation, but on the opposite of balance identified with individuals who happen to be women. Gender specification is qualified to the point of conceptual nullification. The power of the individual woman represented by both writers lies in the strength she embodies against the threatened selfhood of the individual struggling with History.

Garcia's representation of Celia as a matriarch steeped in History and inspired by a vision that unifies Cuba and Spain, while her family disintegrates, mirrors Benítez-Rojo's notion of resistance oblivious to apocalyptic opposites or dichotomies. For all their differences in nationality, age and time, Gustavo and El Lider are the doubled figuration of Celia's personification of love. They exist and are meaningful only through the agency of her gaze. Like her granddaughter's creative transformation of memory into art, she, too, recreates History in her dream of love for Gustavo and El Lider.

The differentiation, then, between self and otherness revived by Berger is erased by Benítez-Rojo and Garcia. Duality for the Cuban writers appears in the form of a historical heritage caught in a process of deconstruction where gender plays a phenomenological role (the *fact* of strong characters being women for both Garcia and Benítez-Rojo, paralleled by the *fact* of biological differentiation of Garcia and Benítez-Rojo) but not an ideological one, as in the contemporary Western feminist discourse.

Chapter Two

The Body as Metaphor: Garcia's *The Agüero Sisters*

In "this certain kind of way," Cristina Garcia's second novel, *The Agüero Sisters*, is a continuation and expansion of the motif of perception in her first novel, and in the design of this book. In words and pictures, *Understanding Contemporary Cuba* is about the body in the perceptual mode argued by Merleau-Ponty: "The theory of the body image is, implicitly, a theory of perception" (206). Under the photographer's gaze, the gazed subjects proffer a way for reading a society.

Cuban society is pictured in this book by appearance, shape, color, contour, caught in a whirl of movement, diversity, and constant process of metamorphosis evoking the aptness of carnival as a descriptive and metaphorical term. A key concern is the nature of truth and selfhood hidden at the same time as signified by images. In both words and pictures, a journey is effected through the gaze and the gazed in an act of decoding a society's collective and individualized body. The image of the carousel reflects the former, while the latter is fixed in the faces of young men and women. If anything, everyday living in Cuba revolves around the body or the *look* of things as a gauge for survival on the level of food supply and consumption noted in the next chapter. For Garcia, the struggle for survival is emblematized by the agency of the body, its commodification for the acquisition of food.

My own approach, interrogating the *look* from a modernist angle, is analogous to *The Agüero Sisters*' focus on the gazed body as theorized by Merleau-Ponty ("Our own body is in the world as the heart is in the organism: it keeps the visible spectacle constantly alive," 203). Garcia remarkably enlarges the formal range of *Dreaming in Cuban,* which was essentially about "ways of seeing," to include a reflection on the ways chosen by her characters to untie themselves from a world seemingly predetermined by their bodies.

With the body as a central metaphor, she provides an organic connection between three generations of women in a single family. Their collective and individual bodies are seen either in moments of timeless fixity or, more often, in instances of scarification induced by History. The two Agüero sisters (Constancia and Reina) and their mother (Blanca) dramatize this duality underlined by the process of fragmentation of History. The daughters of the second generation are foregrounded while those of the third generation (Constancia's Isabel and Reina's Dulce) are backdrop doubles of their mothers. They, too, are defined by their relationship with their bodies.

Garcia's narrative gaze on the body expands *Dreaming in Cuban*'s focus on the gaze itself, but the issues are similar. They concern History, power, perception, gender dichotomization, in addition to selfhood and otherness. Her women characters choose to assert themselves with their bodies, effecting their liberation from presumed pre-determined entrapment.

On one level, Garcia's *body* is the Cuban body politic misruled by a father figure (Ignacio) committed as an ornithologist to the mapping of the land. Ignacio, whose father came over from Spain, is defined by his relationship with natural science and fatherhood; and both stand for the idea of Europe's discovery and settlement of the New World. His endeavors as a scientist and a father are not unlike a Conradian mission of enlightenment that fails when faced with the otherness of Blanca, his young wife, whose own family history (colonial planters of French extraction who fled a slave revolt in Haiti) foreshadows the clash between Blanca and Ignacio. She is the free-spirited individual who for a time escapes her imposed historical and marital bonds with Ignacio. Acting on her freedom, she has an affair with a "dark" native who sires her daughter Reina. Her act of freedom from Ignacio leads to her victimization in the arresting pastoral setting that opens and closes her story. Blanca's freedom and victimization are associated with the virginal, pristine flora and fauna of the New World suggested by her name, Blanca, "whiteness." The words on her tombstone emphasize the purity of beginnings: "In life and death, pure light" (192).

Thus, the body defined against the backdrop of the first generation of Agüeros is the initially revered but ultimately destroyed landscape of the New World. It provides a subtle critique of colonialism in the Conradian and Sartrean context of the dichotomy of self and otherness. The second and third generations' location in the metaphor of the body incorporates a colonial clash that is extended to the contemporary terms of revolutionary Cuba's struggle as a nation against the impact of U.S. domination.

Cuba's isolation as a revolutionary nation is personified by the individuals' sense of entrapment in their bodies. The forms for breaking out of gender subjugation are signified by each one of the Agüero women's choice of self-affirmation as they assert control of their bodies. Europe and the U.S. symbolically relay each other in their own attempted control of the Cuban body politic. The Revolution meant to counteract both forms of colonial domination impacts on individual lives, enlarging their entrapment and search for self-liberation as a nation's quest.

On another level, the metaphor of the body centers characterization. Constancia is the Lourdes-like immigrant to the U.S. who has built a successful business catering to the cosmetic needs of women in the exiled Cuban community. She concentrates on makeup and perfume geared to keeping women young and pristine as her product line, "Cuerpo de Cuba" (["Body of Cuba"],231) suggests. Her business is her own self-expression deceptively mirroring "her mother's face" (105 ff.) as an icon of ageless, youthful beauty. Her reverence for her mother's face represents a biological and mythical (Narcissus-like) adherence to surface appearance which she translates into the marketability of her makeup line. Otherwise, makeup acts as disguise for Constancia's ignorance of the exact circumstances behind her mother's death and Constancia's own "dark" self reflected in her sister, Reina. Like a figurative painter, she makes surface appearance her art form; and it is a repetitive one based on reproducing the replica of her mother's face for the marketplace: "Haven't you noticed how often women destroy pictures of themselves, Reina? Nothing conforms with our private image of ourselves. My products bring back that feeling. The beauty of scent and sensation, the mingling of memory and imagination" (162).

By contrast, Reina's body is made up of fragments of skin grafts subsequent to burns sustained in a work accident (she is an electrician). Her scent is also a "mingling of memory and imagination" of a more ominous nature. It is "smoky" (36), meaning she, too, is the embodiment of her mother, but a different side of her mother, not Constancia's image of her timeless youth. Reina is the charred-like remnant of her mother's destruction by gun fire, and her mysterious near-death electrocution parallels the apparent mystery of her mother's death. Thus, while Constancia's canvas is the whiteness (borne by her mother's name) that is her primary material for decoration and makeover, Reina's is the nearly charred body reconstituted with skin grafts that she preserves in the workplace by fixing brokendown machines.

Constancia works with ingredients in her factory to reconstitute the "body of Cuba" in Miami as a successful commodity. Reina works with tools and machines both in Cuba and the U.S. She symbolically masters the mechanics of a market economy that her sister's cosmetic line merely covers up. Reina defines herself by way of her practical understanding of what makes an industrial society "work." Constancia's self-definition is the imaginary world of success conveyed by makeup and makeover. Her adherence to surface is misleadingly like her mother's "whiteness," disguising hidden truths. Reina dismisses surface. Men flock to her and project onto her their fantasies of lust and power. "You're a goddess!" she is told at one point by an admirer. To whom she replies, "*Caballero*, tell me something I don't know " (166)!

Compared to the standard of beauty upheld by Constancia, Reina is the opposite of the women her sister's products aim at creating. She is more than manly: "five feet eleven, a good four inches taller than most of the men with whom she works" (10). She is Amazon-like, self-reliant and powerful: "The most daring of her colleagues call her Compañera Amazona, a moniker she secretly relishes" (*Ibid.*). She is not only defined by her non-traditional line of work, but also by her predatory sexual appetite: "Often, Reina selects the smallest, shyest electrician in a given town for her special favors, leaving him weak and inconsolable" (*Ibid.*).

The story of the two sisters, then, is about power: how to get and keep it using the body as an active agent of self-awareness, choice and action. They are rivals locked in the mystery of their mother's mysterious death. Constancia has inherited her mother's look of innocence and youth even as it lies behind her murder. Reina takes after her father's aggressive behavior which erupts in a cathartic fight with her sister. But she also takes after her mother's liberated "darker" side in her sexuality.

The doubleness of the sisters in their different attitudes to sexuality (Constancia is prudish) is reflected in the chiaroscuro effect of their different skin colors (Reina is dark; Constancia is light). In fact, they represent the light, surface appearance of Blanca obediently faithful to her scientist husband; and the dark inner self she acts on when she elopes with a lover. The light and dark motif serves as a clue to the reversibility of the sisters' identity connected with their different attitudes toward their bodies.

An additional doubling of light and dark is carried by their daughters. Dulce, Reina's daughter, essentially uses her body as a commodity to make her way out of Cuba (*Sex is the only thing* they can't ration in Havana," 51). It is the same perception of her body that underlies her donating a skin parchment from her thigh for her mother's skin graft. Reina's sighting of Dulce's scar reminds her of her own mother's burns on her forearms as a result of a lab experiment (37).

Isabel, Constancia's daughter, makes pottery and lives in Hawai with her artist boyfriend who uses her body for performance (43). Her brother, Silvestre, is gay; and he kills his father, Gonzalo. Thus all three offspring of the third generation of the Agüeros replicate their parents since their bodies are set in a conflictual or gender-bending form.

Finally, the "gazed body" motif in *The Agüero Sisters* serves as a metaphor for a landscape in ruins. Blanca's killing takes place in the countryside as a hummingbird hovers over her head. Ignacio, her ornithologist husband, "as if pulled by a necessity of nature" (299), destroys that which he cherished: his young wife and, symbolically, the landscape.

As in *Dreaming in Cuban*, the "sins" of the fathers are repeated until the third generation; their "sins" extend Jorge's jealousy of Celia's love for Gustavo in Ignacio's own jealousy of Blanca's "dark" lover. The women's bodies are symbolic of the land subject to devastation by the fathers' misrule. But they are also the sites of regeneration for the daughters who take charge of their bodies. Constancia inscribes her mother's face in the commodity market that her niece, Dulce, similarly makes use of; both relying on the body for self-assertion. Reina, on the other hand, makes use of and exercises control over her body as an instrument (like her work tools) for self-achievement. Her ethic is obviously shared by her daughter Dulce, but also by her niece, Isabel, the only daughter of the third generation to give birth: "Isabel lifts a breast toward her aunt. Reina closes her eyes and breathes in the distant scent of her mother, closes her eyes annd settles her lips on her past" (241).

The woman's gazed body in *The Agüero Sisters* is a shifting image. In one instance, it focuses on the abused, displaced, commodified, made-over woman as an analogue for the spoliated land. In another instance, it portrays the sexually active, iconoclastic, gender-breaking woman who takes control of her life in her own choice for liberation. The woman's body is the Cuban land that struggles for freedom and survival. Cuba, however, is no longer a metaphorical colony (Blanca) subject to a colonizer (Ignacio) whose voice reduces everything to silence. The defining quality of characters like Reina, Constancia, Dulce and Isabel is their differentness masked by the deceptive sameness of gender. Beyond each one's physical appearance is the different individual route taken, building on the heritage of dissidence passed on to them by their mother and grandmother.

Chapter Three

Phenomenology and Photography: *Looking Cuban*

I am not a professional photographer. I used a small, black, Canon "Sure Shot 85 zoom" with a lens range of 35mm to 85mm. I easily slipped it into my pants' pocket or jacket and carried it inconspicuously. When it was noticed by my subjects, I thought the obvious contrast with the more sophisticated cameras around the tourists' necks or their hand-held camcorders saved me from being identified as a tourist. I also knew that my physical appearance worked in my favor as I easily blended with the majority of the people encountered in Havana. It eased up the inevitable tension between the photographer and his subjects. I did not have to work at being part of the scenery and at not being a passive recorder reducing individuals to objects.

Beyond appearance, my thoughts turned to Henri Cartier-Bresson, the French photographer well-known in my youth for the pictures of "ordinariness" he took with a black Leica. The picture that I best recall from *Paris-Match*, the French counterpart to *Life* magazine in the U.S., was his shot of a soldier on a tank kissing a girl during the liberation of Paris. He used a camera not to make photography but to capture "life," as he repeatedly said. He carried it with him everywhere he went as an extension of himself, taking pictures that aimed at representing his sensorial response to the world around him.

That was exactly what brought me to Cuba: my wish to reconnect with my senses after excessively toiling on the computer with the written word. I did not see myself as a passing tourist but as a visitor engaged in a process of revitalization, and I relied on my camera to capture what went into that process.

I, then, had three assets to work with: first, I looked like the majority of my subjects; second, I had a small camera; and, third, my familiarity with the work of a renowned photographer served as an inspiration to capture the everydayness of life. Like Cartier-Bresson, I had my camera with me whenever I stepped out on the streets. Just as I immersed myself in the pulsating life of the city I tried to record scenes involving people that made for that pulsation. And I felt comfortable with an underlying literary purpose when I recalled Ezra Pound's famous definition of the image as an emotion and an idea frozen "in an instant of time" (*Gardier-Brzeska* 86). Cartier-Bresson's definition of photography perfectly mirrored Pound's definition of the image ("the camera is...the master of the instant...that moment that mastering an image becomes a great physical and intellectual joy," *Henri Cartier-Bresson* n.p.).

At some level of sensibility, verbal expression could not be differentiated from the visual. (I quoted the relevant line from Horace's *Ars Poetica* that gave classical resonance to Pound's and Cartier-Bresson's common dictum. "Ut pictura poesis," I wrote on a postcard to a McGill colleague to give him a sense of Havana.) I set out in the city to reconcile visibility and invisibility, as paradoxical or quixotic as this may seem. I strove to erase the distance between subject and object, foreignness and familiarity, self and otherness.

Yet, reaching for the right visual/verbal representation, as articulated by artists of the past, was not really an intellectual agenda. It need not be if I retrieved the truth of my senses and blended with Caribbean life -- after all I was born in the Caribbean. I, too, could use photography as a natural extension of myself (Cartier-Bresson's "way of life," *Ibid.*), a Caribbean man recording his return to island life.

I roamed the city, from the Nuevo Vedado district where I lived to Old Havana, walking through Vedado or Central Havana to the Malecón on the seashore of the city. I crossed over to the Miramar district by car and merely stopped for a couple of routine shots of a setting that seemed to have more in common with Palm Beach, Florida, with its wide avenues, posh houses and lush greenness than Havana. No wonder, as I learned, this is where the rich of the days before the Revolution had lived, with an eye on Florida where they kept or escaped with their fortunes.

Everywhere else in Havana but Miramar drew in my sight, because it is "everywhere else" that the people lived. The revolutionary government had taken over Miramar and turned it into a showcase for the world to witness Cuba's stature as a nation, first by renting the confiscated mansions of the rich to foreign embassies, and also by building a huge Convention Center for international conferences (no less than four of which took place when I was in Havana). Deals were struck with Spanish, Canadian and French entrepreneurs to build highrise hotels connected to the same international resort chains that sprouted in Varadero, Cayo Coco and other places on the island for the avowed purpose of drawing in badly needed foreign currency. Miramar was not meant to be for the immediate benefit of the Cuban population, no more than the resorts.

I looked at the people, and they looked at me in the Vedado districts and in Old Havana. I saw the numerous museums and historical sites in Old Havana. I photographed some of these historical sites (the cathedral), and some of the hotels in Vedado (the Nacional) and on Paseo Prado in Old Havana (the Inglaterra). I also photographed the streets (Salvador Allende, Obispo, Ayestaran, among others). But, mostly, it was the *feel* of these places and faces I tried to capture at noon or at dusk; always feeling the rhythm, the movement, the tactile aliveness of men and women, schoolgirls and schoolboys, *jineteros* and *jineteras* (the hustlers who kept asking "Where are you from? Want to buy cigars?" --until I grew tired and brushed them off, shouting "I am Cuban!"). The streets were the people's living rooms. They moved around like an endless carousel. I felt perfectly comfortable among them because I was living through my senses and theirs.

I locked eyes with brown, black, green, hazel and blue eyes. I heard the music of their street chatter whose syncopation I understood better than the lyrics themselves (Cuban Spanish is notoriously fast paced). From little holes in the wall on Ayestaran, Salvador Allende and Old Havana, I smelled the fried chicken legs, fish cakes and pork cubes, as well as the varieties of homemade pizzas. At times, I could not help but bump against lineups at foodstalls, maybe because I was distracted watching the ingenious making of hero or submarine-like sandwiches out of slim slices of ham and cheese.

People were eating either standing or walking on sidewalks and galleries. "They're always eating," my wife observed more than once. We guessed it was an overt manifestation of a survival tactic in light of food rationing. What was necessary for full and varied meals was limited to chicken and pork, and vegetables when they were available in season at the farmers' markets. Anything else was set aside by the government for the resorts. Yet, no one went hungry, no one looked underfed. Survival meant eating little but at any time during the day or night out on the street.

I did not take pictures of such scenes, no more than I did of the incredible display of grandeur and decay of the old buildings on Salvador Allende and in Old Havana with balconies overrun with clothings left to dry. Looking at these narrow streets, these old and decrepit tenement buildings similar to the one where Sixto lived with his family, I thought of the iconography of time inscribed in these buildings whose replicas I had seen in Naples. They did not need my own recording, except on a couple of occasions.

What I hope the juxtaposition of my pictures of Havana records is the youthfulness, vitality and diversity that makes the city such a visceral, unique experience, giving it a spirit that can only be represented in a congenial form of photography focused on simplicity, quotidianness and organicity.

* * *

Henri Cartier-Bresson was my model, but I am not Cartier-Bresson. My approach to photography rested less on narrative than on the potential reader's gaze locked with mine, merging sight with activities that were communal and inclusive of the gazer and the gazed. That seemed to be the meaning of my use of sequential shots of what I earlier referred to as "the carnivalesque carousel."

In my Portfolio there are, first, the photos of the schoolchildren's celebration of José Martí's anniversary ending with a closing shot of them at recess; and those of an impromptu joyful scene on Ayestaran complete with drums and trumpets. Set in Havana, these shots stand for the whole of the book's use of music as leitmotif. Like a jazz piece played by Chucho Valdés or Gonzalvo Rubalcaba rhythmically and fluidly drawing in opposites like the North American and Latin American musical traditions joined by a common African source, they are repeated by different individuals but convey the same spirit of youthfulness, diversity, and vitality that can be seen in the pictures taken in Santa Clara in the second section.

There, the opening shots improvise on the sighting of tourists in the shadow of Ché Guevara's statue, the follow-up shots are again of schoolchildren, or they capture scenes revolving around Parqueo Central.

The third section, Matanzas, picks up a similar rhythm improvising on the movements of a young couple frolicking in the sea, ending with their sitting in the sand. For some reason, I seem to hear the lyricism of Chucho Valdés's "El Bolero" in the juxtaposition of the sea, their gaze and their youthfulness.

On the other hand, it is "Lácrimas Negras" played by Ibis and her band on the rooftop terrace of the Hotel Inglaterra that I hear in the final section. The shot of the anonymous dancing girl rounds up the carousel of light and shadow. In the darkened setting and the dark figure of the dancer, there is a recurrence of the flashes of light in the opening images on Plaza de la Revolución. Light-and-shadow is a predominant motif that suggests the interrelatedness of apparent opposites at the heart of Cuban society. Seen in the contrast between young and old, fair-skinned and dark-skinned, time past and present, and the pictures taken one morning on Parqueo Central, in Santa Clara, chiaroscuro is perhaps best emblematized in the pictures midway in the book of Elena and her friend smiling in the shadow and then in the light of a restaurant terrace.

Next to musicality, light-and-shadow, and movement, sequencing also means the encircling presence of History. The figure of Ché Guevara is in all the main sections of the Portfolio. It hovers over the Plaza de la Revolución across from José Martí's statue; it stands on guard, as it were, over the tourists coming to visit his mausoleum in Santa Clara; and it looks from a wall below a bridge in Matanzas.

Images of organicity at the farmers' market at Tulipan tie in with the presence of the sea in the closing images of Matanzas. Images of interracial diversity in contemporary Cuba predominate from one end to the other: the opening shots on Plaza de la Revolución match the street scenes in Old Havana, and they are rounded up by the images of Elena and her friend in the Havana section, just as they are also present as a form of closure in the shots of the young couple at the beach in the Matanzas section.

Looking at the pictures, I am also struck by the recurrence of images of transportation in Havana: from the *wawas* (huge camel-like city buses), the fleeting or broken-down old cars, the *cocotaxis* (three-wheel motorcycles that look like hardboiled eggs, with the tops sliced and yellow-colored on the outside), to pedicabs and bicycles. Then there are the horse-driven carts in Santa Clara and the sailboats in the Bay of Matanzas. They suggest the constant movement characteristic of Cuban life.

Palm trees and coconut trees are everywhere in Havana, Santa Clara and Matanzas, and they convey a sense of organicity and reproduction. Not coincidentally, images of youth open and close the Portfolio while they are foregrounded in the middle sections of Santa Clara and Matanzas. That they represent schoolchildren on the whole connote the defining significance of education both for the present and the future of Cuba: the hopeful meshing of learning, discipline, progress and enlightenment.

Education identified as "the battle of ideas" is the slogan I repeatedly heard in the Cuban media. Another one heard in January 2003 was "*Un otro mundo es posible*" in connection with a conference held in Porto Alegre, Brazil, and attended by a substantial Cuban delegation made up of a cross-section of Cuban society. In the broad coverage given to the occasion, I recognized Juan Miguel Gonzalez and his son, Elián (whose picture in the media in the U.S. and Cuba, in 1999-00, centered a moral dilemma that to her credit, Janet Reno, the then U.S. Attorney General, solved with dignity). Yet neither Elian's nor his father's name was mentioned by the TV commentator when they greeted each other at the airport or when they were seen sitting next to each other at the Convention Center when the Porto Alegre delegation was given an ovation in the midst of an international conference on education. The fact of not naming father and son served the State's commitment to socialism: collective solidarity prevailing over individual achievement in the making of History.

That would not be the sole occasion when I witnessed the State's use of imagery for a collective purpose. It was manifest in the ceremony I photographed of thousands of schoolchildren wearing their uniform, led by their teachers on Jose Martí Day. I also sensed the display of power in the way the State stressed education in its pronouncements (the militaristic "battle of ideas" I kept hearing). It left me with mixed feelings which may as well be the lasting impressions of my pictures. There is something frightening for an educator witnessing the molding of minds in the single direction of affirming the "homeland." No less frightening were the speeches of the young and the old uttered by rote, repetitive to the extent of sameness.

I was, however, alert to the distinction between what I heard and read in public, official form and what remained unsaid or said in understated fashion in private. The distinction between official and unofficial discourse suggested a similar duality in the educational process. The freedom to think and speak for oneself is an unalienable, natural right that cannot be impeded and, like the cyclical process of nature itself represented by the young, goes on even if it is in the masked form of ceremonies, uniforms and rote learning.

Mask is surface, and picture-taking represents what can only be seen. The Cuban look is therefore deceptive if meaning rests on surface representation. If anything, the unceasing gaze of the Cuban onlooker is an invitation to a participatory exchange couched in understatement silently conveying meaning that there is more than meets the eye. The onlooker's fixed gaze, like the camera lens, is yet part of a carousel that never stops. The photographer focuses on the carousel while he is wrapped up in a whirl of meaning whose shifting images resist and entice fixity in an instant of time.

Not unlike the photographer, the reader of this book is both an *onlooker* and a *participant* engaged in a journey of discovery that begins with the reflection of things as they are, and proceeds to reflexively suggest what lies behind the face of things. In that sense, we are all "looking Cuban."

Portfolio

Havana

Photo 1

Photo 2

Photos 1 - 3: Schoolchildren at the Plaza de la Revolución on José Martí Day, January 28, 2003.

Photo 4: The parade is over.

Photo 5: A neighborhood in Old Havana.

Photo 6

Photos 6 - 7: Students at the University of Havana.

Photo 8: The Plaza de la Fraternidad in Old Havana.

Photo 9

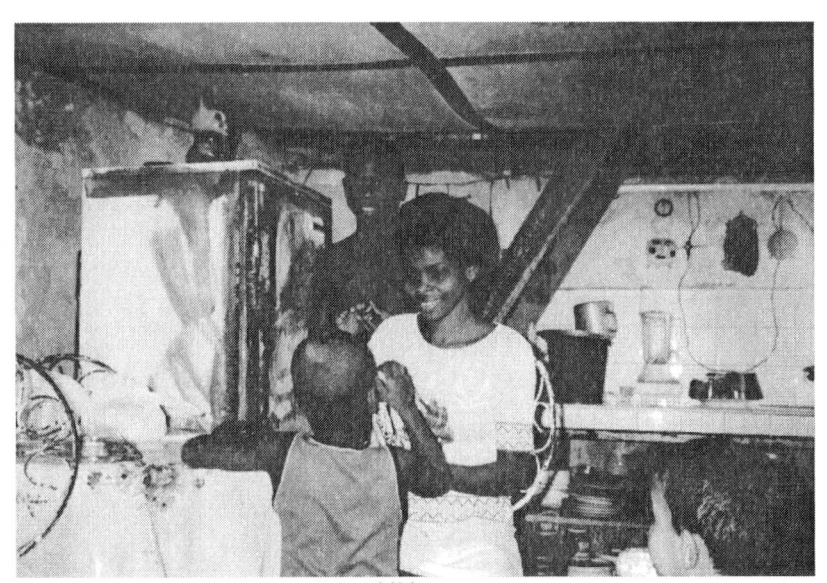

Photos 9 - 10: Sixto, Maria and the children.

Photo 11: Hemingway's favorite bar.

Photo 12

Photos 12 - 13: Two crowd scenes, in each one a shared gaze.

Photo 14: A car breakdown in morning traffic.

Photo 15

Photo 16

Photo 17

Photos 15 - 18: An impromptu band and followers. In each shot someone is engaged in visual dialogue with the photographer.

Photo 19: At the Tulípan farmers' market.

Photos 20 - 21: Elena and her friend.

Photo 21

Santa Clara

Photo 22: Ché Guevara standing guard while tourists come for a visit.

Photo 23: Sandlot baseball game not far from Ché Guevara's mausoleum. It's a hit!

Photo 24: Early morning scene.

Photo 25: Getting in line for morning class at Santa Clara High. One student's arms are crossed and he looks the other way.

Photo 26: Three friends in Santa Clara Square. A tour bus came to a halt, a group of tourists disembarked with their camcorders. They began shooting. The friends laughed. One of them said, "That way they'll go home and say they know Cuba!"

Photo 27

Photos 27 - 28: When the two friends in photo 28 saw the picture of the gentleman in photo 27 being taken, they also asked to be photographed.

Photo 29: A smiling bystander.

Matanzas

Photo 30: The Ché's ubiquitous gaze, now in Matanzas.

Photo 31

Photo 32

Photos 31 - 33: A young couple frolicking in the sea at Matanzas (photo 31); glancing at a sailboat (photo 32); and having their picture taken with their friend (photo 33). The only one fully gazing and smiling has her hand resting on her boyfriend's arm. Their friend looks forlorn. A love story.

Photo 34: A *hombre* without a care in the world, his snoozing lulled by the wind and surf.

Back to Havana

Photo 35

Photos 35 - 36: The old American cars kept running as state-decreed historical landmarks. The bicycle and the *cocotaxi*, a revised three-wheel motorcycle, are also familiar sights in Havana.

Photo 37

Photo 38

Photos 37 - 39: Ibis and her band on the rooftop terrace at the Inglaterra. The two dancers keep up with the rhythm.

Photo 40: "How can we know the dancer from the dance" (W.B. Yeats, "Among Schoolchildren")?

Chapter Four

The Fisher-King's Body: Hemingway's *The Old Man and the Sea*

In Havana I was naturally drawn to look up Ernest Hemingway's favorite watering holes (the *Floridita* and the *Bodeguita del Medio*) and the hotels (the *Ambos Mundos* and the *Valencia*) where, according to more than one tourist guide, he retreated to recover from his drinking. I saw them in Old Havana, but I declined to join the crowd of tourists inside. I took in information about his *Finca Vigía* in San Francisco de Paula and the village of Cojímar he used as setting for his classic novel, *The Old Man And The Sea* (1952). I also made a point of not visiting either place.

My reasons were twofold: first, because of my phobia of entrapment by entrepreneurs who turned legendary figures into tourist attractions (in Santa Clara I saw Ché Guevara's mausoleum but did not go inside either); secondly, because I taught Hemingway's *The Old Man And The Sea* along with his other works set in places like Spain, France, Italy and Africa. I was always fascinated by his ability as an artist to incorporate the concreteness of actual setting with a broader imaginative design where space played the role of an objective correlative for the purpose of characterization and artistic truth. I derived pleasure from seeing how places that I had visited were transformed in Hemingway's vision.

So, as I visited Cuba I gathered enough of the sensorial, tactile perception of setting that Hemingway made use of either in *To Have And Have Not* (1937) or *The Old Man And The Sea*. As well, albeit unconsciously at the time, it may have been my sense of loyalty to his representation of tourists at the end of *The Old Man And The Sea* that determined my attitude toward them in Cuba. A silly remark made about the skeleton of the fish brought back by Santiago ("I didn't know sharks had such handsome, beautifully formed tails,"127) ironically punctuated the epic quality of his ordeal that only he (and the reader) understood. From seeing (and fleeing from) tourists in Cuba traveling in hordes, momentarily turned loose from their enclaved resorts, I surmised their comments would be echoes of what Hemingway put in the mouth of the tourist in *The Old Man And The Sea*. I did not want to hear that again or similar words to that effect. So, I shied away from tourists, especially in places like bars, hotels, the Finca Vigía or Cojímar where they flocked in search of gossip about the Hemingway legend.

However, I savored the feel of the place that inspired Hemingway. Thinking about the gaze as metaphor, I understood how the character of Santiago in his aloneness on the sea and on land, his relative voicelessness and his physical rapport with the environment as a fisherman grew out of Hemingway's deep immersion into Cuban culture. Bradford Sylvester, in "The Cuban Context of *The Old Man and the Sea*," has argued for the Cubanness of the novel evidenced by the father-son relationship between Santiago and Manolin, the baseball references and the myth of the Virgen de la Caridad del Cobre. It seems to me that Sylvester's argument can be extended to include the centrality of looking and the understated use of language I saw at work in Cuba.

* * *

An opening description in *The Old Man and the Sea* refers to Santiago's eyes ("Everything about him was old except his eyes," 10). It signals that the nature of the narrative is embedded in Santiago's relationship with the sea and the fish. His gaze is painful in anticipation of what his body as a whole will undergo: "The sun rose thinly....Then the sun was brighter and the glare came on the water and then, as it rose clear, the flat sea sent it back at his eyes so that it hurt sharply and he rowed without looking into it" (32). The main action with the fish and the sharks takes place at night. Early on, the narrative juxtaposes light and youth, darkness and old age. The light of youth is a painful ordeal that old Santiago is set to overcome: "All my life the early sun has hurt my eyes, he thought. Yet they are still good. In the evening I can look straight into it without getting the blackness. It has more force in the evening too. But in the morning it is painful" (33).

In his encounter with the fish and the sharks Santiago undergoes a transformation: the fish is his double in action and resolution. He sees his youthful body, when he was called "the champion" (70), when the fish emerges from the water (the emphasis is on the sun implicitly containing the association with pain and youth): "He came out unendingly and water poured from his sides. He was bright in the sun and his head and back were dark purple and in the sun the stripes on his sides showed wide and a light lavender" (62). It is that same body, now old, that is reflected at the outcome of the night struggle in the dismembered body of the fish he brings back to shore: "He saw the white naked line of his backbone and the dark mass of the head with the projecting bill and all the nakedness between" (121).

Santiago returns from a journey of confrontation with time past and present. The missing "tinted photograph" of his wife in his shack (16) is an icon of his lost youth. His failure to account for his wife's disappearance self-reflexively evokes a time in his life when he did not "see" things as they were but as he imagined them to be (the tinting of the photograph). But there is more. The photograph of his wife is that of a look that he cannot bear seeing ("it made him too lonely to see it," *Ibid.*). That sense of discomfort accounts for his taking it down, but the photograph is far from forgotten since Santiago knows exactly where he put it ("it was on the shelf in the corner under his clean shirt,"*Ibid.*).

Thus it can be argued that Santiago's wife is a "gazing body" that is hidden and resurfaces in Santiago's journey of expiation gazing at his own body. The device of the photograph introduced early in the novel places a frame on the journey qualifying it as a search for self-understanding externalized by the struggle with the marlin and the sharks. Santiago's body encompasses two time frames: the marlin emblematizes the past, his youth as the arm-wrestling champion --hence his referring to it as his double or "brother" (59)-- then as the marlin is hacked by the sharks the same body is subjected to the ravages of time; and it is the present, and Santiago is an old man. His bloodied hands (99) parallel the blood of the fish drawn by the sharks (103, 110), his tiredness reflects the agony of the fish (112), his understanding of aloneness is objectified by the fish's reduction in size by the sharks: "He could not talk anymore to the fish because the fish had been ruined too badly.... 'Half fish,' he said. 'Fish that you were. I am sorry that I went too far out. I ruined us both' " (115). The image of the ruined body of the fish mirrors Santiago's own ruined body.

There is a double-tier to Santiago's gazing body: the fish, as mentioned, stands for the time of his youth, and the sharks for the passing of time resulting in the dismemberment of the body. In killing the fish and accounting for it in grief and remorse (103, 115), Santiago is rejecting the illusion of youth; and the fight with the sharks represents the passing of time and things as they are (reality). He identified with the fish (his youth) at an early stage and his loyalty to bonding extends to undergoing the ordeal visited by the sharks. His fight with the sharks is analogous of what he did to the fish. The result of that second struggle is his admission of physical destruction. The qualification "...but not defeated" (103), of course, sums up the true meaning of the journey: Santiago's acceptance of his body subject to the assaults of time resulting in the skeleton remains of the marlin.

A singular feature of the gaze in Hemingway's narrative is his use of language as a frame. As many critics have remarked, the novel is narrated in the form of a soliloquy which splits into the imagined dialogue of Santiago speaking to the fish or the sharks. But he is in fact speaking to himself as time is remembered and presently lived with the fish and the sharks. His first-person narrative's shift to the deceptive third-person voice mirrors a less obvious but deeper struggle; one that is masked by the ritual of life and death, man and the environment seen in the eyes of Santiago. What is unseen to him, but that the reader decodes, is the inscription of the struggle with time, self and others in his body.

The question, then, is how does the body's own gazing at itself speak a truth greater than what is surmised by Santiago in terms of physical achievement? Admittedly, there lies a measure of his growth in self-awareness, that the real gauge of success or achievement is in terms other than the physical. He is the one who voices the distinction between destruction and defeat (103). But the reader has been presented with the truer, silent language of the body that Santiago's words cannot match in reliability. That qualification comes out in the leitmotif of his dreaming of his boyhood in Africa, told in the third-person (24, 25, 129), thus begging the larger question of the use of the third-person in the narrative as a whole.

Who is the third-person narrator at a seeming distance from Santiago's first-person? It cannot be anyone other than Santiago unless we assume it is Manolin whose companionship makes him Santiago's youthful alter ego. Manolin is crucially absent during the journey. Thus we can only assume that if he is the one telling the story in retrospective form ("as told to..."), he is narrating what the old man told him. But that linkage is never made in the text. To be sure, working with Hemingway's "iceberg theory," the reader finds plausible ground for making such a connection.

Otherwise, one is left with the actual textual evidence of Santiago's split first-person and third-person narrative as an analogue for the layers of his characterization in doubleness. As earlier stated, this doubleness is represented in the context of time (past and present; old age and youth), space (land and sea), objective correlatives (the marlin and the sharks). It may, therefore, be stretched to include the split in narrative voices doubled by the bodily form of prowess and decline: Santiago as a triumphant arm wrester and a vanquished fisherman.

His bloodied, maimed, fatigued body that lies in his shack in the pose of the crucifixion (he "slept face down on the newspapers with his arms out straight and the palms of his hands up," 122) makes him a sacrificial figure, an icon whose visual representation is more significant than Santiago's verbalization as first-person or disguised third-person. On the other hand, the dilemma addressed by many critics regarding the reiteration of the dream of his boyhood in Africa up to the very last scene apparently makes for an inconclusive, ambiguous ending (whether the journey has been one of psychological growth or one that ends up where it started, with a romantic vision of a world that Santiago never controlled, symbolized by the missing wife or gazing body of the "tinted photograph," 16). The dream of Africa is told in a consistently third-person *voiced* recollection (24-25, 66, 81, 127) that encircles the narrative and adds to its framed form. Therein lies evidence, then, of the inconclusiveness of the ending and the argument for the state of psychological stasis Santiago apparently does not overcome even after undergoing his epic journey.

Yet, the ending also includes the fixed image of his battered body lying face down in bed looking at itself in the pose of the crucifixion. Two scenes are juxtaposed: one is the mute, graphic, Christ-like image; the other is the dream recollection. Because so much insistence is placed in the novel on the language of the body in action or inaction in contrast with the recourse to the language of a split narrator, the image of the body gazing at itself seems to provide a firmer sense of closure. That image punctuates in silence what is at the center of the book, the seven-eights of the iceberg that lie unseen. Every conflict in the book is included in its fixed frame.

The meaning of the narrative demonstrably lies in Hemingway's use of the objective correlative; how the externalized action with the fish and the sharks is a mask for the real nature of Santiago's journey and the appropriate means for its narration. The struggle is the tip of the iceberg. The body gazing at itself through surrogates, masking itself in the ambiguous first-person and third-person voice, cryptically points to what lies unseen beyond language and is alluded to in Santiago's first-person revelation: "A man can be destroyed but not defeated" (103). The literal meaning of that sentence is tellingly obscured by Santiago's subsequent repeated use of the word "beaten": "Now they have beaten me, he thought (112).... He knew he was beaten now (119).... It is easy when you are beaten (120).... 'They beat me, Manolin,' he said. 'They truly beat me' " (124).

* * *

To be sure, an interpretation of *The Old Man and the Sea* based on Hemingway's use of body language is obvious since the novel is overtly about the struggle of a fisherman with the elements. It may lie simply in Santiago's own recognition of the perils conventionally faced by fishermen "going too far" asea. What Hemingway does, however, in a Cuban context is to epitomize a reflection -- in the disguised form of the ancient genres of allegory or epic-- on the theme of survival in a primal state. That may well be the central theme of his work as a whole; and *The Old Man and the Sea* is its point of ultimate achievement.

Hemingway's last novel represents the completion of a vision which he articulated theoretically and put into practice throughout his creative work. It is part of an aesthetic based on his wariness of conventional language and preference for the objective correlative of setting, action or image that not only speaks for the emotion that cannot be described but for the truth of vision: *"...what the actual things were which produced the emotion that you experienced...the real thing, the sequence of motion and fact which made the emotion"* (*Death in the Afternoon* 2. Italics added). For instance, in *A Farewell to Arms*, he comments about place names having dignity (185). "Dignity" is the noun he uses to describe his iceberg theory of understated writing in *Death in the Afternoon*: "The dignity of movement of an ice-berg is due to only one-eighth of it being above water" (192).

In *The Sun Also Rises*, Jake Barnes silently carries the burden of a maimed body, and he struggles to find the words matching Pedro Romero's skills as a bullfighter ("...his purity of line through the maximum of exposure," 168). In *For Whom the Bell Tolls*, Robert Jordan envies Pilar's gift for storytelling ("God, how she could tell a story.... I wish I could write well enough to write that story," 134) linked to her connectedness with an elemental culture ("But you had to have known the people before. You had to know what they had been in the village," 135). In *To Have and Have not*, Harry Morgan works and speaks like a gangster. And he loses an arm. His representation is fixed in his maimed physicality culminating in the long descriptive scene of his Christ-like agony on the sea, bleeding to death. Cerebralness, conventional, proper language, are the butts of satire. Marie, his wife and widow, articulates what Harry Morgan stood for. Her refusal to attend his funeral is predicated on her preference to remember: "His goddamn face.... Everytime I see his goddamn face it makes me want to cry" (128).

Throughout his writings Hemingway used the body as metaphor for what Philip Young termed "the wounded hero" (*Ernest Hemingway*). The many stories and novels where violence is foregrounded have been accepted as valid representations of times and places in a state of war. The artist's choice to depict characters and events in visual and oral language served a moral purpose, one that amounted, for art critics like Emily Watts and Thomas Hermann, to verbal variations on the Goyaesque iconography of "the agony of man."

In *The Old Man and the Sea*, Hemingway revisits the Cuban setting, and Cubans, of the thirties of *To Have and Have not*. A world of extreme violence is transformed and transcended in an arena of elemental nature rendered by the aloneness of a single individual, the mythical figure of the Fisher-King reenacting the rituals of life and death. Santiago's iconography also incorporates the range of archetypal heroes in the Western tradition, i.e. Christ, Ahab, Lear, the Ancient Mariner, and any number of representations of the individual hero caught in the act of creation or re-creation of a physical ordeal. The bruised, maimed body of Christ, Ahab, Lear or the Ancient Mariner is replicated in Santiago's.

More readily, in a Cuban context, Santiago's body is a fusion of the African and Spanish past, and American present, that makes him the architect of his destiny that in the end need not make the promised pilgrimage to the Virgin of Cobre (16). His sea journey has indeed been a reenactment of the legend of the Virgen de la Caridad del Cobre described by Benítez-Rojo (*The Repeating Island* 11-15). Found on a boat off the Cuban coastline that carried her from Africa and Europe, she became the founding myth of a nation made up of Africa, Europe and America.

Santiago's gazing body is a refraction of three continents joined in the formation and survival of the Cuban nation. Robert Jordan's wish to write as well as Pilar told a story comes to fruition in Hemingway's last novel set in a place "...he had known before" (*For Whom the Bell Tolls* 135).

Chapter Five

Looking for the Light: Walcott's *Collected Poems* and *Omeros*

Hemingway is twice mentioned by name in Garcia's *Dreaming in Cuban* (178-179; 220). Derek Walcott, in an interview, spoke of Hemingway as "the only one to let you see the Caribbean the way it is, to feel it and smell it....No one has written about it better" (*Critical Perspectives on Derek Walcott* 398). And he also referred to him as one "of the two great Caribbean artists" (*Ibid.*) he was thinking of while writing *Omeros* [the other was Homer].

Both Garcia and Walcott indicate that their writing is inscribed in a Caribbean literary continuum that appropriates Hemingway as "our own," in García Márquez's words (*Hemingway in Cuba* 7). [In the penultimate chapter I address Edmundo Desnoes's radical dissent from García Márquez and other admirers. In *Inconsolable Memories*, he categorizes Hemingway's legacy as one of colonialism in Cuba while ironically showing Hemingway's influence on his own writing style. *Author's note.*] Walcott demonstrates in *Omeros* how his use of the sea, the figure of the fisherman and the act of fishing are amplifications of the roles they play in *The Old Man and the Sea*.

In the closing chapter I suggest a connection between a Cuban Elena and Derek Walcott's Helen through their respective gaze. For now, I would like to propose a discussion of Walcott's poetic work as a variation on the motif of the gaze linking him to Hemingway and Garcia as Caribbean artists whose works refractedly address the myth of origin, or the creation of the body seeded by the contraries particular to the Caribbean.

Though Garcia and Hemingway anchor their stories in Cuba and Walcott centers his work in St. Lucia, all three writers appropriate the Caribbean sea as a personified body in an individual's look. Celia's whole life, for instance, in

Dreaming in Cuban, is contained in the opening image of her standing on the seashore and watching. Constancia, in *The Agüero Sisters*, recreates the Cuban body with a cosmetic line called *Cuerpo de Cuba* (129) inspired by her sighting of her mother's face. Santiago's story, in *The Old Man and the Sea*, begins as a summary of his life at the crossroads: the fact that "he had gone eighty-four days without taking a fish" (9). As a result of his traveling to Cuba, Walcott wrote a poetic sequence ("Tropic zone," in *Midsummer)* that reflected his disenchantment with a setting characterized by images of incarceration, sterility and the deadening use of language. Yet, the image of the body in need of nurturing that he shares with the other writers is the metaphor for incorporation central to his poetic work.

* * *

Asked to comment on the concluding line of the signature poem in *Sea Grapes*, "The classics can console. But not enough" (*Collected Poems 1948-1984* 297. Unless otherwise indicated, the poems quoted are from this collection), Derek Walcott replied, "The truth of human agony is that a book does not assuage a toothache" (*Partisan Review* 213). That response, steeped in paradox, simultaneously using and questioning the power of language to affirm the primacy of sensory experience, constitutes a central trope in Walcott's poetic discourse. It is epitomized in the cathartic encounter between the narrator and his mentor in the resolution of *Omeros*: "A girl smells better than a book.... A girl smells better than the world's libraries" (7. 56. 3). The "girl" is Helen ("I remember Helen's smell." *Ibid.*), and she is symbolic of St. Lucia, the poet's birthplace, and its people ("Love is good, but the love of your own people is / greater," *Ibid.*). The terms of the epiphanic journey in *Omeros* are, therefore, characterized by the use of metaphors designed to elicit a sensorial texture. Such an emphasis in Walcott's masterwork suggests the importance of retracing the poet's use of impressionism throughout his early and late work. In a larger, deeper sense, Walcott's use of language to affirm the primacy of sensory experience emerges from reconciliation between two initially antithetical poles: the Western literary tradition and a New World aesthetic.

Rei Terada argues, in *Derek Walcott's Poetry*, that it is wedded to a paradigm of "mimicry" whose premises are stated in "The Caribbean: Culture or Mimicry?" A close look at Walcott's essay suggests the extent of Terada's misreading of the poet's use of irony in rejecting "mimicry" or imitation as a valid course for New World writing: "Because we have no choice but to view history as fiction or as religion, then our use of it will be idiosyncratic, personal, and therefore, creative. All of this is beyond the sociological, even beyond the 'civilized' assessment of our endeavor, *beyond mimicry* [italics mine]" (*Critical Perspectives on Derek Walcott* 57).

Against "mimicry's" fatal flaw, Walcott believes that the New World experience compels originality and freshness in the use of language. An Adamic vision thus informs much of his poetry: "Creation," "Invention," "Beginnings," are words that he interchangeably uses otherwise in his essays to convey his commitment to the New World:

> For every poet it is always morning in the world.... There is a force of exultation, a celebration of luck, when a writer finds himself a witness to the early morning of a culture that is defining itself, branch by branch, leaf by leaf, in that self-defining dawn, which is why, especially at the edge of the sea, it is good to make a ritual of the sunrise. (*The Antilles* n.p.)

Much before his 1992 Nobel Prize lecture, from which this quote is taken, Walcott repeatedly stakes a claim on the appropriation of language and its incorporation into the felt experience indigenous to the New World. To Edward Hirsch, for example, he substantiates, and simplifies, the Adamic vision first proclaimed in his 1974 essay, "The Muse of History," as "this elemental privilege of naming in the new world" (9): "I have felt from my boyhood that I had one function and that was somehow to articulate, not my own experience, but what I saw around me" (*Critical Perspectives* 72).

Omeros has been assessed as the culmination of Walcott's self-avowed quest. The consensus among critics validates the long poem's rewriting of the Homeric epic for a fresh rendering of the Caribbean experience (*Ibid.* 396-399; 400-403. See also Jervis Anderson's essay in *The New Yorker* 78). The poet who, in "The Muse of History," had early on rejected the epic as a "literary project," if it meant the distancing effect bred in the genre and the poet's concurrent attitude toward his subject, demonstrates the consistency of his thinking when, in the wake of *Omeros*'s critical acclaim, he tells D. J. R. Bruckner: "I do not think of it as an epic" (*Critical Perspectives* 396). To another interviewer, Jervis Anderson, he elaborates by quoting from "The Muse of History": "I believe, as I've said elsewhere, that the epic poem is not a literary project. It's already written. It is written in the mouths of the tribe" (Anderson 78). This deconstruction of genre is made imperative by Walcott's sense of urgency to inscribe his voice in a communal continuum whence he derives strength as a person and legitimacy as an artist. Thus, he further tells Anderson, "And I felt that I had been chosen, somehow, to give it voice" (*Ibid.*). A note of gratitude is echoed in the two interviews. To Anderson, Walcott says, "I was writing it for the island people from whom I come. In a sense, I saw it as a long thank-you note" (*Ibid.*). To Bruckner he adds: "What drove me was duty: duty to the Caribbean light. The whole book is an act of gratitude. It is a fantastic privilege to be in a place in which limbs, features, smells, the lineaments and presence of the people are so powerful" (*Critical Perspectives* 396). The linkage between gratitude or pride in origin and a sensory evocation of the poet's sense of self and collective identity is furthermore correlated with a reference to "light," a dominant metaphor in Walcott's mature work.

What this complex and revealing statement signals are some key elements that counterpoint the dominant, canonical aesthetic of "the classics" Walcott subverts. Juxtaposing his poetics and his poetry in his early and late development suggests that Walcott's contention with the canon revolves around the dichotomous, polarized, hence incomplete, range of "the classics" for the New World artist. They have addressed the "head" and not "the body," to put it in clear, simple terms similar to the poet's. The classics can only "console"; they do not "heal" or prevent "ailment," it is implied, because they are unresponsive to the visceralness of felt experience. The New World poet, molded by the concreteness of time and space unknown to "the classics," is thus condemned to invent and create from that specificity: "Perhaps the only privilege that a poet has is that, in the agony, whatever chafes and hurts, if the person survives, produces something that is hopefully lasting and moral from the experience" (Montenegro 213).

* * *

In this discussion I aim at taking up Walcott's challenge to assess his work as a verbal journey in felt experience particular to the New World. My argument will be developed along three intersecting lines: first, the recurrent figures of Odysseus and Helen seen as conflicting icons in the poet's journey through linguistic abrogation and appropriation; second, a set of metaphors associated with birthing and nurturing tied to the sea that are identified as integral elements of a self-reflexive, unfolding creative discourse; third, how these metaphors cohere within a "delayed decoding" construct wherein Walcott integrates a canonical form of impressionism in a quest for pure aesthetic.

Admittedly, Walcott is not the first New World or Caribbean poet to successfully challenge tradition. He himself provides a context that is clearly genealogical when, in "The Muse of History," he singles out Aimé Césaire and St. John Perse, respectively from Martinique and Guadeloupe, as his closely related forebears. They are praised for their pioneering effort in deconstructing the metropolitan language and making it responsive to the Caribbean in a changed vocabulary and texture evocative of its felt specificity:

> I do not know if one poet is indebted to the other, but whatever the bibliographical truth is, one acknowledges not an exchange of influences, not imitation, but the tidal advance of the metropolitan language, of its empire, if you like.... It is the language which is the empire, and great poets are not its vassals but its princes. (*Is Massa Day Dead?* 15)

Walcott's perception of these two poets obviously mirrors his own beliefs. His aesthetic, like theirs, is not exclusionary but complementary; it is not imitative but innovative; it is historically grounded in a metropolitan language that has been transformed by indigenous control and experience.

As early as *In a Green Night* (1962), Walcott uses the Homeric figures of Odysseus and Helen to dramatize his quest for an authentic Caribbean expression by subverting the classics. They are positioned in an aesthetic of division best identified by "two Helens": "Between two Helens,/ yours is here and alive" (*Omeros* 7.62.2). At the outset of his journey, he admits to alienation: he is alternately drawn by a European and a Caribbean iconography. The poet is the wandering Odysseus figure, irresolute and ambivalent, and he is reflected in the problematized images of Odysseus and Helen. This starting point is crucial for a middle stage in his development, introduced by *Another Life* (1973), seasoned in *Midsummer* (1984) and stressed as "the heat of home" in *The Arkansas Testament* ("The Lighthouse," 1987). A tactile identification of place conveying the poet's sense of the Adamic newness of the Caribbean yields a metaphoric language for its creation, appropriating the biological process of birthing and nurturing. The poet's mature work, exemplified by *Omeros*, conclusively points to an impressionist aesthetic of "home" or the New World whose tone and texture centrifugally resolve the earlier tension between the binaries of alienation and authenticity.

* * *

The first stage in Walcott's journey can be seen in two poems from *In a Green Night*: "A Map of the Antilles" and "Roots." "Map," a lament for the stillbirth of the West Indian Federation, draws a parallel between the distorted vision of Caribbean politicians and the poet's. Against the prevalent myopia of both ("men invent those truths which they discover"), the idea of "home" or homecoming is aborted when alienation prevails. In contrast to the apparent, but deceptive, benign surface image of the sea, Odysseus's journey symptomatizes the extent of uprootment: "Even as he lingered in Circean seas; /...in no magic port was there such peace / As where his love remained." The specificity of language, landscape and identity is buried for the alienated poet and the politicians under the illusory recourse to universalism that makes "a mockery of the heart."

"Roots," on the other hand, makes a more emphatic claim for clarity of vision: "...till our Homer with truer perception erect it, / Stripped of all memory of rhetoric." The need to articulate the truth of the Caribbean experience is yet made difficult by the weight of colonial history. History, misread and misunderstood, is the colonial's burden long after colonialism has officially ended,

Walcott argues in "The Muse of History." "Roots" illustrates this point in the dispossession of language: "When they conquer you, you have to read their books." The poet's task is a difficult one, for he has to abrogate a received tongue (starting with a substitute for Homer) and appropriate it as well for his own use. "Sorcière," therefore, reflects the native topography in need of foregrounding, in contrast to the inculcated reflex of a search for validation involving Switzerland. The point is that the New World topography is self-referential, as should be its language severed from Old World inscription. Walcott addresses, then, the key issue of language specificity for innovation in poetic form. The implications of "naming" are further explored in "Roots" when the focus turns to Vigie and Helen.

The former, a main peninsula off Castries, St. Lucia's port city and capital, is juxtaposed with "Helen, old Helen lying alone in bed." There is a close parallelism between the two: "St. Lucia's colonial history is embossed in its being named 'Helen of the West Indies'." In "Leaving School," a 1965 essay, Walcott writes:

In elementary school we had been taught that Saint Lucia was "The Helen of the West" because she was fought for so often by the French and the British. She had changed hands thirteen times. She had been regularly violated.... Her name was clouded with darkness and misfortune; Columbus had named her after the blind saint; her saint's day was December thirteenth. Even her natural history was tragic. (*Critical Perspectives* 24)

St. Lucia's status as an object of predatoriness is coded in the alien resonance of classical taxonomy. Helen reflects Europe's self-image while Vigie connotes the Caribbean's self-reflection. As the site of the lighthouse illuminating Castries' harbor, it symbolizes the possibility of self-identification inscribed in language arising out of the meeting of the New World sea and land. The promontory's colonial history ("the ageing wall," "the stone turrets" and "the yellow fort") is tempered, if not canceled, in the poem's resolution by the metamorphosis of Odysseus as "an old fisherman" framed by the elements, "rowing home in the rain." Odysseus changes from the aimless wanderer to the poetic persona of the survivor, the colonized subject, who can yet be the "prince" of his fate if he understands that "from all that sorrow, beauty is our gain."

Walcott's revisitation of history is voiced in a cautionary discourse qualified by doubleness or tension between opposites in "Roots." The history of the Caribbean, he suggests, remains an alien one as long as it is written by others. Its true history, on the other hand, is a challenge to indigenous creation. Yet both, the existing and the yet-to-be-born versions, have to be recognized --the latter as the antithesis of the former. The doubleness of Homeric allusions in Walcott's work is fundamental, then, for his strategy of reaching for a synthetic vision. An initial stage in that project stems from subversion of the dominant, canonical nomenclature. The re-creation of Odysseus as an old fisherman illustrates the poet's intent. Redefined by the ritual of fishing, Odysseus's canonical status is deconstructed and the terms of his redefinition are introduced.

A predominant symbol in Walcott's later poetry is the ritual of fishing that concludes "Roots," and it is emblematic of the poet's conception of the rootedness of his craft in his native space. As an everyday practice defining the islander's relationship with his environment, fishing is proposed as an apt analogue for post-canonical poetry indigenous to the New World. The poet-as-fisherman identifies the connectedness of the writer with his birthplace; it is a trope for authenticity. The "lines" of the poem are closely related to those cast by the fisherman as gauge for value. In "Nearing Forty," a 1969 poem, the poet states: "You will rise and set your lines to work / ...until the night when you can really sleep." In "The Schooner Flight," published ten years later, the narrator says: "Well, when I write / this poem, each phrase go be soaked in salt; / I go draw and knot every line as tight / as ropes in this rigging." In *Midsummer*, finally, the anticipation of *Omeros*'s subversion of an epic of gods and warriors yields the poet's choice of analogy for his craft: "You could map my limitations four yards up from a beach --/ a boat with broken ribs, the logwood that grows only thorns,/ a fisherman throwing away fish guts outside his hovel. / What if the lines I cast bulge into a book that has caught nothing" (xxix).

"Roots" conclusively augurs of "that light beyond metaphor" sought in *Omeros* (6.54.3). Yet, before that latter stage is successfully reached, the weight borne from "the classics" conjures up the dominant gloomy representation of Odysseus and Helen in Walcott's early poetry. As the burden of colonial history, theirs are images of dispossession, alienation and hopelessness, "borrowed ancestors" seen as a challenge to native invention. Helen, for example, is not only one of those "ancestors" in "Homecoming: Anse La Raye" (1969). She is Janie, in *Another Life* (1973), "the town's one clear-complexioned whore"; while in "Menelaus," from *The Arkansas Testament*, she is dismissed as "the white trash that was / Helen.... A whore's." Similarly, Odysseus, in "Homecoming: Anse La Raye." discovers "there are no rites / for those who have returned... there are homecomings without home." As well, his return home, in "Sea Grapes," is to a land of "gnarled sour grapes," one that "brings nobody peace."

An albeit faint and fragile reversal appears in "Map of the New World," when the "old fisherman" of "Roots" is now a "man with clouded eyes" who "picks up the rain / and plucks the first line of the Odyssey." The association of age, rain and motion points to a self-reflexive affirmation. As in "Roots," it positions Odysseus as the poet-as-fisherman on the threshold of reclaiming his natural home. Helen appears also as an aged, changing figure whose maturation suggests growth in the same poem ("Helen's hair, a grey cloud").

A more substantial manifestation of change occurs in the symbolism of "light." In the two poems --"A Map of the Antilles," and "Roots"-- from *In a Green Light*, light is blinding or uncertain, and certainly less than a reassuring presence. The light of the "emerald sea" in the first one is associated with excess and lack of control ("wild...destructive ocean"); in the second, natural light is unpleasant ("The hard coral light which breaks on the coast"). The artificial light implied in connection with Vigie's lighthouse intensifies, on the other hand, the fragility of the closing line's reference to age and rain. Developed further in a subsequent poem like "Homecoming: Anse La Raye" (1969), it is menacingly seen as "this sheer light, this clear, / infinite, boring, paradisal sea." The gloomy journey home in "Sea Grapes" (1976) opens with the ominous image of "that sail which leans on light." In all these instances, light is in fact "darkness" or absence of vision, blindness, dispossession. The poet wears a false, deceptive mask of illumination like Helen/ Janie's hair in *Another Life* (1973), "black/ hair electrical."

With *Midsummer* (1984), however, the image of light is transformed and accompanies a changed, youthful, natural Helen. The insufficiency of "the classics" is recalled; the "new" Helen is unlike the "old" Helen since she is "not Nike loosening her sandal" (xxv). She now represents a sensory investment in language tied to the landscape of "home." Foreshadowing her representation in *Omeros,* the poet allies Helen with the Caribbean light: "like a candle / flame in sunlight." The poet's altered Odysseus figure, the fisherman, finds enlightenment in his mirrored double, Helen, who legitimizes "[the] palms [that] have been sliced by the / twine / of the craft I have pulled at for more than forty years." His craft is embedded in the endless ritual of island fishing; "home" is thus incorporated: "the lines I love have all their knots left in." In addition to ritual, the poet's craft now partakes of clear vision. It is symbolized by Helen who is the natural light of "home." The Helen identified as "here and alive" in *Omeros* (7.62.2) is imagistically defined in *Midsummer*: "Then, in the door light: not Nike loosening her sandal, / but a girl slapping sand from her foot, one hand on the frame" (xxv).

Midsummer represents a turning point in Walcott's poetics. It links in arguably significant ways his early and late poetry. Odysseus and Helen evolve from figures of sterility to fertility, from symbols of alienation to identification, and from the distancing of language to its appropriation. The symbolic journey they exemplify is from death to life when Odysseus's return to a land of "dead / fishermen" in "Homecoming: Anse La Raye" is contrasted with its felicitous counterpart in *Midsummer*.

* * *

The relationship with the sea provides another perspective on Walcott's developing poetics. Incorporation correlates with genealogy and the sea is used as a prismatic metaphor for the appropriation of the biological process of birthing and nurturing as self-reflexive poetic discourse. In *Omeros*, for instance, the poet evokes his father's words: "Simplify / your life to one emblem, a sail leaving harbour / and a sail coming in" (1.13.2). This to-and-fro movement objectifies the poet's unceasing search for truth and accurate vision that resists fixity. It further strengthens his identification with the "new" Helen whose embodiment of light progressively reveals itself, as the poet unburdens himself of canonical dependence.

Emergence of New World invention, as earlier suggested, takes the form of the perception of Helen as the native muse, in *Midsummer*. She stands for more than a literary cliché when she is a defining, genealogical trope for self and collective identity: "But to curse your birthplace is the final evil" (xxix). The metaphorical range of that line is explored by the poet; first, in response to a direct question from Edward Hirsch as to its intent, he states: "I think the earth that you come from is your mother and if you turn around and curse it, you've cursed your mother" (*Critical Perspectives* 80). Then, in *Omeros*, the same idea is maintained but the reference to the sea is added to complete the metaphor: "A man who cursed the sea had cursed his own mother. / Mer was both mother and sea" (6.45.3). The genealogical trope is thus all-encompassing; "voice" unites the male and the female life forces, even if it is a male speaker's who asserts root identity in the birthing process. He *names* the truth of his self and creative identity. But the masculinity of perception and expression is made subservient to the creative *process* linking land and sea, and whence it originates. The act of creation, the *birthing* of the text, then, is analogous to motherhood while, as the above quotes indicate, the male speaker's self-identity is subordinated to the "femaleness" of birthing and place: both the earth and the sea are *mothering* entities.

It is within such a complex symbolic construct, fusing creativity and self-identity and their accompanying textual, biological and psychological implications, that Helen plays the role of a unifying, revitalizing figure reflecting the poet's developing consciousness and control over his craft. By *Midsummer*, she is the emerging *light* beyond cultural alienation. The fusion of the self and the land she represents ("the girl slapping sand from her foot") culminates with its amplification in *Omeros*. The speaker first sees her "easing straps from each heel" (1.6.1), then he specifies that "her clear plastic sandals swung by one hand" (1.6.2); thus, attention is drawn to Helen's contact with the land with her bare feet.

The connection between Helen's feet and the land emblematizes the authentification of craft and language the poet associates with genealogy. His father is remembered for foreshadowing Helen's relationship with the land in a telling instance, when the sight of peasant women walking uphill brought the admonition: "They walk, you write... and your duty / from the time you watched them from your grandmother's house / is the chance you now have, to give those feet a voice" (1.13.3). The tactile relationship between feet and land parallels the correlation between sight and light. In either instance, it reveals an evolution in understanding dramatized by the reiteration of Helen's duality in two poems from *The Arkansas Testament*.

The classical representation of Helen as whorish, in "Menelaus," counterpoints her prototypical significance in "The Light of the World." Though the mythical resonance is obviously biblical in the latter poem's title, a very secular meditation on guilt and the search for expiation dominates thematically. Three women figures symbolize the terms of the dilemma: "Helen" (not named but related to the named one, in *Omeros*; they both share a yellow piece of clothing, a feline and ebony analogy and a mesmerizing quality), the speaker's mother, and a marketwoman. A connection is made between the first two figures, starting with the juxtaposition in the speaker's thought process:

> I looked at two girls, one in a yellow bodice
> and yellow shorts, with a flower in her hair,
> and lusted in peace...
> That evening I had walked the streets of the town
> Where I was born and grew up, thinking of my mother
> with her white hair tinted by the dyeing dusk. (49)

Just as Helen, in *Omeros*, resists reification in the conflict of male desire between Achilles and Hector, she plays a similar (albeit more enigmatic) role involving the speaker and an implied Hector in the ominous van in "The Light of the World." On the other hand, her power as subject in control of life-giving (her pregnancy) enhanced by her knowledge of the expected child's father's identity (compared to Achilles' and Hector's ignorance) is problematized here, even as in both poems she exercises control over the poet's creativity. The dynamic of creativity at risk in the earlier poem, linking the speaker and "Helen," is further externalized by the marketwoman's address to the van: "*Pas quittez moi à terre*" (*Ibid.*). The poet doubly dwells on the multiplicity of meaning contained in the use of Creole, the maternal vernacular. On the one hand, the land ("*terre*") and air (the van named "Comet," in *Omeros*) are opposed; on the other hand, "Helen" and the speaker are fugitives in contrast to the marketwoman's and the speaker's mother's ties with the land. The conflict between home and exile is given a new twist.

The speaker's presence on the van is as ambiguous and threatening as the van itself, when Hector's fate is considered as one of its implications in *Omeros*. Here, deceptiveness prevails, at least on the surface, for everyone is involved with the vehicle and its purported symbolism of progress. The speaker's presence on the moving vehicle traveling from Castries to Gros Ilet, from a port city to a fishing village, alludes to his returning journey "home" from a creative standpoint, to the vision he initially ascribes to "Helen" and to a fuller one identified with his mother and the marketwoman. His return is contextualized by a sense of guilt that underlies surface deceptiveness. The speaker's progressive raising of consciousness is ironically externalized by the vehicle's movement and its ultimate destination (Gros Ilet, the fishing village, presumably "Helen's" home as well as the poet's) that is never reached in the poem. (Gros Ilet is the principal setting in *Omeros*, and its centrality is foreshadowed in an eponymous poem in *The Arkansas Testament*. A pattern of revisitation of a similar setting is quite frequent in Walcott's work; its function is to signal how perceptual growth parallels poetic development. For instance, "The Lighthouse," also in *The Arkansas Testament*, is a mature reflection on the symbolism of the Vigie lighthouse in the earlier poem, "Roots.")

The surface images revolving around the van added to the speaker's assertion of homecoming as reinsertion into his community ("I wanted to be going home with her ["Helen"] this evening," 50), prove to be false in light of his gnawing feeling of guilt: "I had abandoned them, / I had left them on earth" (51).

Truth and vision are imperiled on the van: yet, the image of "earth," with the surface and hidden meanings of the marketwoman's use of the vernacular the speaker scrutinizes, is other than simple as it points to the speaker's own paradoxical state. The journey motif closes on an apparent note of retribution, linked with the theme of guilt. The incompleteness of his journey, noted by the speaker's echoing words, "they left me on earth" (*Ibid.*), suggests retribution and expiation compounded by validation of the marketwoman's fear of abandonment, in one instance.

But the "earth" image, as earlier noted, is complex: it may mean rootlessness *and* rootedness, depending on perception or point of view. Thus, the speaker's rejoining the ground at the end of the poem may stand for a counter, affirmative stance tied to the genealogical tropism of earth and its life-giving feminine symbols (the speaker's mother and the marketwoman). The poem, in very concrete imagistic ways, then, turns on reflection, perception and mirroring; and it sets up their challenges in the deceptive allusion of its title to a mythical, canonical source. "Light," here as mirror, is meant to reflect the complex complementarity of selves inside and outside the van. "They left me on earth" would therefore carry the alternative choice of rootedness for the speaker rejoining the genealogical community of his mother and the marketwoman, in contrast to the technological one of the van fraught with menace hovering over "Helen."

Two visions are opposed and extend to the land and its future: one is alluring, and it is the mirage-like effect of technology circumscribing "Helen," and it is sterile like the van's incomplete journey; the other counters the false light of technology. It is hidden in the "shadows" associated with both the speaker's mother ("with her white hair tinted by the dyeing dusk," 49) and the marketwoman ("the Market / itself was closed in its involved darkness / and the shadows quarreled for bread in the shops," *Ibid.*). The complete form of the journey lies in joining "Helen's" "carved ebony mouth" (48) with the other women's communal "shadows" ("I, who could never solidify my shadow / to be one of their shadows," 50). The speaker leaves unsaid in the end the terms of this reconciliation. It is even left hovering in a menaced form over "Helen" who is still on the van. His own disembarking from the van implies a personal reconciliation, and the poem's self-reflexive claim on authenticity in vision --but the relationship sought between the self and the community represented by "Helen" remains unresolved.

The alluring and problematized image of "Helen," in "The Light of the World," points to the duality of her iconography in Omeros: "These Helens are different creatures, / one marble, one ebony" (7.62.2). While Julie Minkler ("Helen's Calibans") correctly notes the appearance of ambivalence in the lines that follow ("each draws an elbow slowly over her face / and offers the gift of her sculptured nakedness," *Ibid.*), one is valued over the other, even as (and maybe because) her actual namelessness in "The Light of the World" reinforces her exposure to false vision, and her fragility is the speaker's own struggle on a journey whose real terminal point is in *Omeros*. Then, she is substantiated by name (Helen), she rejoins the earth (the van and Hector are at a distance) and, principally, she iconizes the completeness of the journey in Gros Ilet, the fishing village where she works as a nurturing figure (whether as a domestic at the Plunketts or as a waitress at the Halcyon hotel). In *Omeros*, she is definitely the "light" sought by the speaker though it blinds him initially, and he is faced with the task of achieving vision beyond the blindness of metaphor.

"Helen's" distance from the earth, implied by the marketwoman's cry, in "The Light of the World" (*"Pas quittez moi à terre"*) is bridged by Ma Kilman in *Omeros*; her niece is a rejuvenated Helen. The *mothering* appropriation of the earth that completes "Helen's" identity is introduced otherwise in Walcott's earlier work dominated by a male speaker intent on foregrounding genealogy and the centrality of its feminine process for his own creativity. Thus the marketwoman's cry is, in fact, an echo of the speaker's exclamation in "Sainte Lucie" (1976): "*Moi c'est gens Ste Lucie. / C'est la moi sorti; /* is there that I born" (*Collected Poems* 314). A filial point of view confirms the maternal, and they fuse for the purpose of stressing the birthing process of the self and the poem.

A broader context for genealogical tropism and Helen's ultimate meaning in

Omeros as "that light beyond metaphor" (6.54.3) lies in the call for "the style past metaphor" linked with "the household truth" in the 1969 poem, "Nearing Forty." That form of truth is given substance in the ordinary lives of Gros Ilet, in *Omeros*. The deconstruction of language ("past metaphor") sought in the poet's early and late work is achieved by means of simplicity and clarity in diction associated with the *household* paradigm. The weight of the classical canon is discarded: "But I saw no shadow undermine my being /... I was seeing / the light of St. Lucia at last through her own eyes" (7.56.2). The "Homeric shadow"(6.54.2) of tradition, Old World aesthetic, is replaced or subsumed by the Adamic stamp of beginnings, implying the construction of "home" where the self and the elements are one: "to see Helen as the sun saw her" (*Ibid.*).

The rapport between the poet and Helen rests on a process of gestation akin to the freshness of language of New World invention. Accordingly, the sea's omnipresence plays a vital role when it is inscribed in the vernacular of St. Lucia that does not phonetically distinguish between *mer* and *mère*, as noted by the speaker more than once in *Omeros* (1.2.3; 6.45.3). But there are further implications to the sea's "motherhood" in the semiotic deconstruction of the word "Omeros." The middle syllable's double meaning is framed by beginning and closing syllables that visually evoke a circle. All three syllables conflate, consequently, as a vast encircling motif charting the form of the narrative as a journey resisting closure; and one which also blurs the boundaries between the supposed opposed female and male principles of sea and land. Dichotomizing these principles is a legacy of the Old World canon, and this form of shortsightedness is recognized by the narrator's mentor, the canonical "Omeros," near the end (the "book" vs. "smell" antithesis *he* draws, 7.56.3). Closer to New World truth is the narrator's mother's joining of the two when referring to his father, Warwick, as "Nature's gentleman" (3.32.1). The narrator, in "Sainte Lucie," identified as a son, completes her perspective beforehand when, in response to his self-articulated plea, "Come back to me, / my language" (*Collected Poems* 310) he resorts to the maternal tongue, Creole, to affirm, "*C'est la moi sorti*" (*Ibid.* 314).

Not surprisingly, the social and historical terms of the journey in *Omeros* are dominated by masculine, wandering figures seeking to exercise control in one form or another over others or the environment. Major Plunkett, Achille, Philoctète, Seven Seas, and the narrator are thus linked by a common Odyssean streak which even overshadows the shipwrecked Crusoe typology noted by Edward Hirsch ("Robinson Crusoe was [Walcott's] first, and indeed his most persistent, symbolic figure for the West Indian artist," *The Georgia Review* 31. See also Walcott's own essay, "The Figure of Crusoe," *Critical Perspectives* 33-40). That the "male" form of their journey is self-destructive and sterile, the narrator's own account, in *Omeros* and elsewhere, makes that clear in the figure of the unreconstructed Odysseus. But that the culture-bound concept of maleness itself is called into question is an undercurrent throughout Walcott's poetry that is fully highlighted in the genealogical construct that formally privileges the femininity of creativity.

Nature, Adam's realm, is emphatically feminine in the poet's work. The problem is not the commonplace quality of such a tropism. As previously discussed, it lies rather in separating the "worn out" trope, deadened by tradition, from a "fresh" one necessitated by New World invention. Birthing and nurturing metaphors are enlisted to meet this challenge, and the archetypal image of "home" or, in the poet's words, "the household truth," provides the anchoring frame.

Next to the womb-like emblem of the name itself when deconstructed ("O-mer-os"), its formal content is built as a series of concentric circles which "maternally" envelope the narrative. The sea, for instance, encircles the island / earth: "The sea moves round an island" (7.58.2). The self-reflexive implication of the text itself is immediately added: "to circle yourself and your island with this art" (*Ibid.*). Another reflexive circle follows in connection with the bird imagery that ties Maud Plunkett's embroidery, Achille's journey to Africa, and the text as a whole, when the narrator notes: "I followed a sea-swift to both sides of this text" (7.63.3). The narrator's internalization of his father's observation on the symbolism of a boat's to-and-fro movement (1.13.2) is reiterated on three other occasions (4.36.3; 6.44.2; 7.64.1). The use of repetition emphasizes the circularity of an activity whose island quotidian quality parallels the natural, visual form of a pattern Walcott associates, with the feminine aesthetic of mother and home in *Another Life*: "I can no more move you from your true alignment, / Mother, than we can move objects in paintings" (*Collected Poems* 157). Indeed, an aesthetic of order tied to stability and place is very much what is remembered by a number of male, wandering characters, like Seven Seas, who echoes the narrator's words in *Another Life*: "You have learnt no more than if you stood on that beach / watching the unthreading foam you watched as a youth, / ...the right journey / is motionless" (7.58.2).

Ultimately, then, the function of circularity in *Omeros* serves an aesthetic of open-endedness in the pursuit of clear vision and expression. It locates its model in "the household truth" given order by the likes of Maud, Ma Kilman, the narrator's mother ("Teacher Alix" in "Sainte Lucie," *Collected Poems* 312), and even Helen as an expectant mother. The space of "home" is contrasted with that of "exile," even as the former might suggest a form of confinement and the latter the "open" space of travel. The real meaning of the journey, as Seven Seas tells the narrator (7.58.2), lies in the discovery of true form, which was there all along in the "home," but alienation and blindness due to "borrowed ancestors" prevented its perception. Divestment of "the classics" means the ability for the narrator to celebrate the New World in the analogue of the home of his upbringing and his true mentor in the figure of his mother: "Your house sang softly of balance, / of the rightness of placed things" (*Another Life, Ibid.*).

Not unexpectedly, "Sainte Lucie," the poet's birthplace named in the vernacular Creole, is placed at the exact center of *Sea Grapes*. The implication is the relatedness of setting, creativity and language to its *mothering* source. (Ma Kilman, who reappears in *Omeros*, plays a pivotal role in "Sainte Lucie." She is the storyteller in the Creole half of the poem.) Notable for its prismatic evocation of an aesthetic of the senses listed in the original Creole names for places, flora and fauna, "Sainte Lucie" highlights linguistic doubleness (Creole and English) as another variation on genealogical pairing. Creole is the mother tongue, and English is, obviously, the father tongue (conspicuously stressed in *Omeros*, when the narrator's father is named "Warwick"). The subtle, visceral and cerebral qualities conveyed, respectively, by Creole and English inform the narrator's mother's reference to Warwick as "Nature's gentleman." The same duality is addressed in "Sainte Lucie" when the narrator's identification of "home" takes the Creole form of "*C'est la moi sorti*" followed by the dialectal English, "Is there that I born" (*Collected Poems* 314). The violation of linguistic propriety --of the "gentleman's" code-- serves the purpose of an intended bridging of the gap between Creole and English by means of dialectally infusing the visceralness of femininity of the former into the cerebralness of masculinity of the latter. Creole's sensorial attributes are identified with the tactile process of the womb in the contrasting use of the word "*sorti*," in Creole, and "born" in English. The Creole language further suggests emergence from the earth itself, an association that is dwelled upon in the narrator's musings about the phrase "*pas quittez moi à terre*," in "The Light of the World." The narrator deliberately pauses on the different meanings in English of the marketwoman's utterance. But whether she means "don't leave me on earth" or "don't leave me the earth," or even, more accurately, "don't leave me stranded" (*The Arkansas Testament* 50-51), the point stressed in the repetition of the word "earth" is the pivotal, gravitational pull of identity linked with birthplace.

An additional parallel between the two poems arises from the symbolism of "light." As previously seen, "light" is embedded in paradox in "The Light of the World." As prism, it is deceptively contextualized by mythology, whether of a biblical or technological nature. It falsely mirrors surfaces while its true location is in the "shadows," i.e. the earth shared by the marketwoman and the narrator's mother to which he returns. The narrator's ambiguous articulation of his return, "they left me on earth" (*Ibid.* 51) is counterbalanced and somewhat clarified by the centeredness of the naming and positioning of "Sainte Lucie," a poem that precedes "The Light of the World."

An implicit connection underlies the narrator's bilingual identification with birth and his birthplace. Birth is tied to "light" or the process of being born to "light" in a specific earthly place (Sainte Lucie) whose name has a Latin root ("lux") that means *light*. Borrowing from another root source (the French undertone to the vernacular Creole "Sainte") completes the mythical resonance of the poet's birthplace: it means *Holy*. St. Lucia, then, stands for *Holy Light*. Being born in St. Lucia is equated with acceding to clear, sacred vision. As with "The Light of the World," the function of mythic resonance is to strengthen the aesthetic of genealogy, birthing. No less significant, of course, in "Sainte Lucie" is the nurturing of language embedded in landscape and the "shadows": "Evening opens at / a text of fireflies" (*Collected Poems* 311).

Yet another variation on the metaphor of birthing is accomplished in a later poem, "Early Pompeian" (1981). A woman's miscarriage serves as analogue for the miscarriage of art and artistic identity. A transition poem of the poet's middle period, its title stands out in sharp contrast to "Sainte Lucie's": it signals a European place name as the point of departure for the rule of entropy. It paradoxically focuses on the antithesis of destruction of the life-giving process for the dramatization of alienation, guilt and the search for expiation --a theme shared with "The Light of the World." Like that poem, which it predates, its real intent is to delineate the terms of true creation.

On the surface, the poem's confessional, personal evocation of a tragic event in the life of a couple, who lose a child to stillbirth, is given the dramatic, historical backdrop of the destruction of a famed city by a volcanic eruption. The paradigm of a *man-made* construct is structurally counterpointed by an act of nature that is ironically creative in itself, but destructive for "others." Clearly, such an oppositional frame signals a range of polarities revolving around a relationship such as the marital grounded in the dialectic of self and otherness. The poem is about the failure of harmony or communication between dualities, and the burden is borne by the self-speaking voice of the narrator whose sense of guilt is further stressed by voicing the "other's" tragic experience for which he bears responsibility. The symbolism of mirrors is again being used in a number of ways; for instance, the self-reflexive meditation on the use and the questioning of language all at once when the experience is sensory and visceral. Hence, the closing, haunting line: "Pardon. Pardon the pride I have taken / in a woman's agony."

The duality of the personal and the historical allows the poet to reflect once more on his doubleness in regard to the Western canon and New World invention. The reference to a mythical city and its destruction infers a self-revealing meditation on lost artistic beliefs. The poet reintroduces the metaphor of stillbirth --first used in "A Map of the Antilles"-- to characterize the failure of vision and language that made him an accomplice of the politicians' distorting "universalism" in the earlier poem. His indulgence in false, derivative or unnatural art leading to the kind of disruption alluded to in "The Light of the World" finds its objective corrlative in the unnatural disorder of a stillbirth. His own delayed or distorted *mothering* of a true text is symbolized by the woman's failed motherhood.

In "Early Pompeian," then, as is the case throughout much of Walcott's work, the maternal trope plays an objective role in the representation of the poet's meditation on his work. If here the would-be mother viscerally bears the speaker's burden in intensely graphic fashion, the risk involved in indulging a form of stereotyping is more than counterbalanced by the concrete display of the poet's consistency in discourse that is both self-reflexive and self-scrutinizing. In other words, the "other" mirrors the self. If perception focuses on the "other," it is in accord with the by now accepted use of the objective correlative for a clearer, unemotional sense of self. The failed mother figure self-reflexively represents the artist's "bad" art. As icon ("You resembled those mosaics"), she merges with the "marble" Helen, and the Pompeian context reinforces the classical canon. Her complexity, however, lies in that she is the product of the speaker's indulgence in canonical myth-making. The personal tone of the poem conclusively suggests that a false, artificial iconography has been imposed on a person, and the result of blunting her naturalness --and telling of the speaker's insensitivity or blindness-- is the miscarriage, the malfunction of the birthing process.

The historical volcanic eruption provides an expanded metaphor for nature's rebellion, the disruption of the woman's self. But before catharsis of a sort is reached and leads to the poem's resolution on an affirmative note, the focus is kept on the "woman's agony" --the features of an artificially-imposed identity. The imagery is relentlessly dark, brooding and deathlike: "Past the lowering eyes of rumors, / ...Now you walked in those heel-hollowed steps / in which all of our mothers before us went." Violation of nature is a sacrilegious denial of the sacred life-force. Religious connotation, as in other poems, is used to assure resonance for the otherwise natural process: "into the lava of the damned birth-blood, / the sacrificial gutters."

Culpability is ascribed to the misuse of the paternal language of empire (the Roman), architecture ("mosaics," "colonnade," "white columns," "stone"), and even technology (the hospital, "scientific" setting) that fails the natural experience of mothering the child / text: "The lamp that was struggling with darkness was blown out / by the foul breeze off the amniotic sea." Art ("the lamp") is denied because creativity ("the sea," the maternal process) is defiled by false language ("the foul breeze"). Blackness, as in earlier poems, is a metaphor for blindness or false vision: "The black harbour, / ...black schooners / ...the sea / is black."

What hope there is grows out of the speaker's raised consciousness. In his witnessing of a stillbirth there is an implied exorcism of his guilt, the practice of a false aesthetic. In the end, he turns to the faint but now understood "light" of the lost child ("little star") and what it augurs of a new beginning, the possibility of true invention in a New World landscape, the turning to the natural, maternal earth. The lost child is "a curled seed sailing the earth." Mainly, the raised consciousness of the speaker is divested of false history and mythology and, in the characteristic fashion seen in the affirmative resolution of similar poems of guilt and catharsis, it blends with the native environment, insisting on the predicates of present time and space: "So I go on / down the apartment steps to the hot / streets of July the twenty-second, nineteen / hundred and eighty, in Trinidad, / amazed that trees are still green."

An intensely confessional poem, one whose subject initially singles itself out by its emotional charge, "Early Pompeian" is nonetheless inscribed in a continuum of abrogation of the canon and appropriation of language and experience specific to the New World. Part of its merit grows out of its juxtaposition with "A Map of the Antilles," which predates it by some twenty years. Both are united by the oblique strategy of focusing on an antithesis to the natural process to validate a New World aesthetic based on fresh invention and symbolized by images of conflicting false and real creations charting the text's development.

* * *

Finally, Walcott's overall design --that of effecting a verbal journey in felt experience-- cannot but integrate his awareness of the aesthetic of impressionism in the Old World with the specificity of New World invention. In the range of early influences, two stand out as they circumscribe the tension between the visual and the verbal arts, and their ultimate fusion in his artistic development. (For an excellent analysis of the relevance of painting in Walcott's poetry, see Robert Bensen, Robert D. Hamner and Rei Terada's works listed in the bibliography.) As the poet puts it, in *Another Life*:

> Where did I fail? I could draw,
> I was disciplined, humble, I rendered
> the visible world that I saw
> exactly, yet it hindered me, for
> in every surface I sought
> the paradoxical flash of an instant
> in which every facet was caught
> in a crystal of ambiguities...
> ...I lived in a different gift,
> its element metaphor. (*Collected Poems* 200-201)

The tension is between the visual impression of Cézanne and the verbal compression of Conrad, and they both use an impressionist texture that strikes a responsive chord in Walcott. The evidence of his awareness of their works is impressive. To Edward Hirsch, Walcott says: "The painter I really thought I could learn from was Cézanne.... It's as if he knew the St. Lucian landscape --you could see his painting happening there. There were other painters, of course,...but I think it gave me a lot of strength to think of Cézanne when I was painting"

(*Critical Perspectives* 68).

Walcott refers to Cézanne by name in a number of poems, particularly *Another Life*, *Midsummer*, and *Omeros*. More importantly, the texture of his poetry repeatedly conveys a Cézannesque play on the senses: "With all summer to burn, / a breeze strolls down to the docks, and the sea begins" (*Midsummer* iii). Crucial to both, Cézanne and Walcott, the image draws attention to its centrality and to the purity of its sensorial quality. A visual focus on balance, color and pattern anchors the quest for an aesthetic of form, order and truth.

As well, Walcott's debt to Conrad is fully acknowledged. He, too, is mentioned by name in *Another Life*, "Volcano," and *Omeros*. Key Conradian motifs (Africa, "fog," "mist," a Marlovian self-reflexive narrator, the use of chiaroscuro) are strewn throughout Walcott's early and late work. As with Cézanne, the important point is Walcott's incorporation of Conrad's aesthetic into a verbal construct that appeals to the senses. Therein lies the resolution of the divided claims of *Another Life* (quoted above). Against the purely visual, and daunting, plastic form of his early trials with painting, he finds a balance in Conrad's use of a verbal equivalent to visual impressionism. Moreover, he extends Conrad's use of perceptual effect in prose expression by means of "delayed decoding" in poetic form (for example, the initial "blinding" appearance of Helen in Book 1 signals the narrator's trial with the true language called for by setting in *Omeros*, one that he does not succeed in articulating --"that light beyond metaphor"-- until the resolution of his journey, in Book 7). And he finds in the New World setting an inspiring analogue to Conrad's use of the tropics in his fiction. Speaking to Bruckner, Walcott substantiates the connection: "I learned a lot in writing the poem [*Omeros*]... the solidity I felt behind me [singling out Conrad's prose] was the solidity of prose. I wanted the feel of great prose rather than a strong verse line" (*Critical Perspectives* 398). Walcott recognizes in Conrad's style, as defined by Ian Watt, "the verbal equivalent of the impressionist painter's attempt to render visual sensation directly" (*Conrad in the Nineteenth Century* 176).

Conrad, then, is a primary model in two ways: first, for his fusion of

Cézanne's style in verbal form, and hence his solving an early dilemma faced by Walcott; and, second, for foreshadowing Walcott's own fusion of the demands stemming from a New World aesthetic revolving around language, setting and characterization, and their claim on the senses.

As it has been argued throughout this chapter, Walcott's poetics is characterized by an aesthetic of doubleness. Nowhere is this more apparent than in *Omeros*'s linguistic structure, which not only blends the appearance of verse (the Dantean *terza rima* and the Homeric hexameter) with the "solidity" of prose, but also, and as subtly, gives extended form to the mixture of a maternal, vernacular language of the people (Creole) and a paternal, distant language of History (English) introduced in poems such as "Sainte Lucie" and "The Light of the World." In the latter instance, Walcott consciously expands on the achievements of his predecessors, Césaire and St. John Perse, he pays tribute to in "The Muse of History."

The orality of the villagers' everyday speech in *Omeros* sharply contrasts with the encoded, scripted language of History. The gap between the two is yet another arena for conflict over control of Helen pitting Major Plunkett against the narrator, on the one hand; and, on the other hand, the narrator against his own rapport with the text. Is it to be "open," like the villagers' voice or "closed," like the Major's language? The latter's limitation for the New World experience is reflected in Plunkett's inability to write the island's history. His failure is directly attributed to his linguistic code's distance from the felt reality of Helen, best understood by his wife, Maud: "Those lissome calves, / that waist swayed like a palm was her island's weather" (2.23.3). Maud, as an artist working with material indigenous to the New World environment (her use of the sea-swift, for example), is perceptually closer to the sensory speech of the people. In the "open" book of the living sound of village life that she partakes in, she represents the reversal or rewriting of history that includes her in the narrator's concern for New World invention, but excludes her from her husband's "closed," unfinished book (and maybe her death reflects its "dead-endedness").

As the narrator, puts it, "Plunkett, in his innocence, / had tried to change

History to a metaphor, / in the name of a housemaid; I, in self-defense, / altered her opposite" (6.54.2). For the narrator, Helen sums up a "natural" frame of reference; one that links orality and identity. After announcing her pregnancy, her not knowing "for who" is ironically transcribed as onomatopoeia, sound instead of concept: "'For who,' she heard an echoing call, as / with *oo's* for rings a dove moaned in the manchineel" (1.6.1).

The narrator's own attitude toward his craft oscillates between the "open" and "closed" form of language use (respectively Creole and English), and he subtly incorporates them into the uniqueness of a text inscribed tonally and textually in the felt life of the villagers (or, as the writer puts it, "the mouths of the tribe," Anderson, *Ibid.*). He identifies the "closed" code as derivative of the Homeric "shadow" that needs the transforming openness of "light." Though its epitome is the sun merging with Helen, the appeal is not only to sight (thus its initial blinding quality in the person of Helen, 1.6.3), but "light" also echoes the Conradian doubleness of meaning contained in his use of sight as a metaphor in the preface to *The Nigger of the 'Narcissus*. Beyond the physical meaning of sight, there is also its meaning as understanding or consciousness. The "delayed decoding" significance of Conrad's "*to see*" serves to substantiate the moral and lasting value of experience beyond the canonical.

Yet, another implication of Walcott's use of "delayed decoding" in the context of linguistic duality is the attendant dialogism within the text's linguistic components and the consequent assumption of reader response --all of which serving *Omeros*'s deep meaning. First, the reader's enlistment in the life of the village is ensured not simply by the centeredness of setting but by the careful weaving of linguistic pluralism, and the symbolism of fishing. The reader reads a text written on the whole in English. Only a delayed effect of the reading process reveals the "real" code beneath the textual surface. Inscribed within the metaphor of fishing, the relationship between the reader and the text is one where he or she is "reeled in" by the submerged, maternal tongue, Creole. The reader comes to the text with pre-conditioned reflexes shaped by the dominant, canonical code of English. The intent, akin to the text's subversion of tradition for the purpose of fresh invention, is to reverse the built-in presuppositions (represented in *Omeros* by Major Plunkett, obviously) so that the deflation of sighting / reading the familiar, reassuring English code leads to the "unseen" part of the iceberg: the *hearing* of the people's everyday, oral, maternal tongue, Creole. (The "iceberg" naturally refers to Hemingway's theory of writing. Another affinity between Walcott and Hemingway becomes manifest. *The Old Man and the Sea*, as mentioned at the outset of this chapter, is surely the Hemingway text Walcott has in mind in his comments to Bruckner [*Critical Perspectives* 398]. Both writers' evident use of the Caribbean sea and fishing for symbolic resonance in their works includes, as with Conrad, Walcott's adaptation of a technical feature associated with prose in order to "solidify," as he says, his poetry.) What Walcott referred to, speaking of Conrad's prose, translates into the "feel" or the "solidity" of the "tribe's" speech hidden by the canonical code.

"Delayed decoding" here means the writer-as-fisherman "baiting" the reader with his lines, "reeling in," "catching" and simultaneously making him or her complicitous in the ritual, thus "landing" the reader into the core of the fishing village, Gros Ilet --the text's mirroring texture. The interplay with the reader's senses is induced by the encircling nautical imagery, beginning with the dedication: "For my shipmates in this craft...." A result of the reader's discovery of being placed in a structurally passive role of being lured by the poet / fisherman is an expected counter-reaction, an active resistance, in fact, that leads him or her to identify and question the manipulative use of language.

If images, metaphors, symbols, linguistic doubleness are lures or "lines" designed for a purpose controlled by a sort of predator, then the reader cannot but be alert to the existence of an agenda built on the nature of language and its user. The poet making use of linguistic artifice expects the reader to awaken to language that calls attention to itself. Thus, the overall strategy of *Omeros*'s use of a dominant linguistic code has the delayed function of revealing its artificiality, on the one hand; but, on the other hand, it points to the truth in hinting at the hidden meaning of things: the endurance and resistance of the villagers, their unheralded nobility akin to their maternal tongue denied official encoding but contaminating in tone, rhythm, texture, and even silence or apparent inarticulateness (like Helen's) the text's relationship with English.

Pure expression lies behind the mask of language's deceptiveness. The poet's intent is to "reel in" the reader in the act of deconstruction and join him in entering "that light beyond metaphor." Pure expression lies in the previously unseen, the purification of "the words of the tribe," a variation on a precept whose Mallarméan and Eliotesque overtones are ironically intended by the poet. As early as "The Muse of History" there is a direct reference to Eliot and a discussion of the Mallarméan "mots de la tribu" cunningly paraphrased as "the mouths of the tribe," a phrase which Walcott repeats in later interviews with Bruckner and Anderson. (See *Is Massa Day Dead?* 9-10)

Helen's cryptic use of language --"Girl, I pregnant, / but I don't know for who" (1.6.1), and "Is the music / the people I like" (2.21.1)-- points to another intended effect of linguistic deconstruction combined with "delayed decoding": the evocation of the deep resonance of a hidden natural language sensed in Helen's sensuality. Her characterization, along with the sea's and Ma Kilman's, merges with the role played by landscape. Then, in Ian Watt's words, delayed decoding "combines the forward temporal progression of the mind, as it receives messages from the outside world, with the much slower reflexive process of making out their meaning" (Watt 175).

Helen iconizes the text's real language in her fluidity of movement (she is a "panther"), balanced form (she is "an ebony mask"), mesmerizing gaze that redefines language ("that incredible / stare that paralyzed me past any figure of speech," 1.6.3), and her sheer embodiment of sensorial oppositional power to the merely verbal (implied in her simple language, "Is the music / the people, I like"). In a way, she is everyone's "shadow": Achille's, Hector's, Major Plunkett's, Maud's, and the narrator's, a mirror for each individual's fractured, incomplete vision bounded by language vainly put to use for her attempted control.

As "that light beyond metaphor," she represents that instance of pure expression ultimately grasped by the narrator, one that language can only hint at *and* where it stops: "Why not see Helen / as the sun saw her, with no Homeric shadow...?" (6.54.2). That the narrator eventually reaches that called-for epiphanic state --"I was seeing / the light of St. Lucia at last through her own eyes"(7.56.2)-- serves to confirm the deeper language of the senses, communion with the elements. In other words, the *beyond language* point sought by the narrator's quest "beyond metaphor" is signified by Helen's "light." She represents the pure expression or pure art of the New World; she is the sun itself, the text's crowning epiphany of self-sufficiency and self-referentiality. The art form she stands for is in no need of outside reference (Major Plunkett foremost, of course; but, as well, the narrator who relinquishes the power of communication to her because he perceives the essence of beauty in her --another variation on her stare that leaves him speechless).

Walcott's statement to Bruckner in reference to *Omeros*, that "the greatest character is the Caribbean Sea itself" (*Critical Perspectives* 398) supports the symbolism of the sea as the outer circle of a series of concentric motifs whose hub is the island. These previously discussed patterns visually function to suggest "delayed decoding." Their delayed meaning is shaped by the perspective on a narrative's true meaning understood by Marlow in Conrad's *Heart of Darkness*: "The meaning of an episode was not inside like a kernel but outside" (30). In other words, the "shell" or outer covering is privileged over the "kernel," the core.

If meaning lies, for Conrad's deceptive narrator, not in the expected storyline or plot but in what is left unsaid or obliquely stated, then it follows that the ebb and flow movement of the sea eloquently contains the overall Marlovian meaning and open-endedness of *Omeros*. The sea's unceasing and enduring process naturally identifies itself as an apt analogy for the mothering and nurturing of the text. Thus, when the narrator confides, "Let the deep hymn / of the Caribbean continue my epilogue" (7.64.1), he merely punctuates the semiotic centeredness of the sea and the endlessness of artistic form modeled on its rhythm that passes for closure in *Omeros*: "When he left the beach the sea was still going on" (7.64.3). The text's qualification of closure parallels the sea's fluidity and externalizes the reader's involvement with its delayed, deep meaning: the moral and lasting quality of the experience.

A marked feature of Walcott's thinking is its affinity with Hemingway's as interpreted and quoted by Bruckner: "He has a special affection for Hemingway because 'he is the only one to let you see the Caribbean the way it is, to feel it and smell it' " (*Critical Perspectives* 398) -- an affinity that is rooted in the Conradian stress on the senses, *seeing, feeling and smelling*, the two writers share. The reader is, then, incorporated into the closing image of Achille's "unthinking" at the end of the day. He or she has symbiotically partaken of the ritual of fishing, the ongoingness of the sea and the textual journey in felt experience that Walcott set for himself.

Finally, not to be overlooked in the enveloping construct of setting and characterization is the role played by Ma Kilman. Her power as healer derives from her inscription in the island's flora. Her mothering relationship with the earth allows her to cure not only Philoctète's physical wounds but Major Plunkett's psychic disarray following Maud's death (6.49.1; 7.61.1). The "new" Helen in the person of her niece completes her mothering range that even subsumes Helen as her tactile rapport with the earth additionally hints at the text's grounding in the specificity of birthplace.

Firmly rooted in the Caribbean earth of his birth, Walcott progressively approximates and successfully articulates in *Omeros*, his masterwork, a counter New World poetic discourse as an alternative to his early perception of the insufficiency of "the classics." His disagreement with the Western canon --its misuse in the New World-- expressed in both his essays and his dour images of Odysseus and Helen in his early work, is overcome in language grounded in sensory perception (impressionism), paced for intended effect ("delayed decoding"), and constructed to impress the texture of "the heat of home." Refracted, Walcott's gaze is no different from that of other writers such as Garcia and Hemingway who propose in their works a less than obvious, but resonant meditation on the myth of origin in the Caribbean.

Chapter Six

Carnival in the Waste Land: Iyer's *Cuba and the Night*

Set in Havana, Pico Iyer's *Cuba and the Night* was published at a time (1995) when he could hardly have failed to acknowledge the Hemingway legend kept alive in landmarks such as the *Floridita, Ambos Mundos*, and the village of Cojímar (7; 8; 81; 197; 208). As well, he probably borrowed a leaf from Cristina Garcia's *Dreaming in Cuban* (1992) by using letter-writing as narrative device and naming a central character Lourdes who, like her namesake, is an ironic reference to a pilgrimage site in France. Both Garcia and Iyer's Lourdes escape from the island. The former becomes an American success story; while the latter changes into a British matron.

Iyer astutely sets up a first-person narrator, Richard, as a photo-journalist in whose pictures of individuals and urban landscape the story unfolds in carnivalesque fashion. (Richard's first two trips to Havana are during Carnival. He lures Hugo, his British friend, to come with him to Santiago at carnival time. And Iyer's essay on Cuba, in *Falling Off the Map*, bears the title, "Elegiac Carnival 1987-1992," 48). The make-believe world of carnival where things are not what they seem --"Even the simplest things are complex here," Richard says early in *Cuba and the Night*, 55-- is undoubtedly the underlying motif of a narrative that dwells on purpose on festivities and behaviors outside the conventional, official norm of an authoritarian society. Given the extensive use Iyer makes of the carnival motif, he is clearly alluding to Bakhtin's conceptualization of carnival as a paradigm for popular dissent (*Rabelais and his World* 9-10).

Everyone, we are told, wears a mask (189-190). And the principal characters in particular (Richard, Lourdes, José, Hugo, Caridad) are defined by their conscious or unconscious disguises, while the plot itself turns on a subterfuge (Richard engineering a bogus marriage between Hugo and Lourdes) that escapes the artificer's control. Picture-taking functions as the prime agent of a carnival-laden world. From an early stage in the narrative the truth of picture-taking is relativized, much like Lourdes's identification as a prostitute, José as a pimp and Richard as a truth-seeking journalist. In his own words, Richard says: "I'm not thinking of the future: my job involves catching the moment. Right now, the here and now, the truth of this instant" (94). A world traveler ("So I went and shot South Africa for a while, Beirut, Belfast, El Salvador: all the garden spots," 86), he sees himself in the tradition of Cartier-Bresson (*Ibid.*). His character flaw is precisely tied to a failure of vision related to his misunderstanding of his craft ("People tell lies, images never do," 19). While he seemingly frets about the morality of making a living off picturing disasters (5), he resorts to clichés to justify his work ("I don't make the news; I just record it," 116).

Lourdes, his loved one, is his foil who repeatedly tells him to face the truth ("That is your job. You make money out of misery....What you see is not the truth; it is Richard's truth," *Ibid.*; "You say you are showing the truth, but it is only the truth you choose," 145). José's father echoes Lourdes: "...pictures won't show you anythin' in Cuba. Everyone here is wearing a mask" (189-190). And to Hugo's "So you believe only what you see?" (191), he replies with sophistry: "Right. Only what I catch with my camera. It's not the whole truth, maybe, but it's true at that moment" (*Ibid.*). Predictably, the breakup of his relationship and the ironic reversal of the marital route he charts for Lourdes's escape from Cuba is in the end directly tied to his blind use of the camera. The pictures he took of Lourdes's friend, Caridad, became commercially successful. Lourdes sees them in a British magazine, recognizes in Varadero the similarity in setting when *she* was the target of his camera. Lourdes's challenge of Richard's infidelity in the end closes on the larger issue of his moral hollowness that motivates her choice to stay with Hugo (232).

Thus Iyer develops in Richard a participant and agent in a carnivalesque world he fails to control or understand, which is analogous to the practice of his craft which he misunderstands. The clichés that he uses as defense are not sufficient to disguise the moral responsibility involved in picture-taking; especially when he claims to belong to Henri Cartier-Bresson's tradition whose pictures aimed at representing "life." In light of his photographs of Caridad, he is instead engaged in an act of deception and profit-making (which, of course, raises questions about his shoots of world disasters).

On the other hand, Richard is also a journalist in the mold of Hemingway's Jake Barnes, in *The Sun Also Rises*, who is constantly torn between the Parisian bar scene and the calling of his craft. However, where Barnes was sexually impotent and therefore forced to turn to his writing as an escape or solace from his bar-hopping and terrace-clinging friends, Iyer draws a contrasting picture of Richard who talks about his work but mainly lives his life in Havana in bars and brothels, and escapes to Varadero and other venues in pursuit of sexual escapades with Lourdes (which he deludes himself into thinking as "love").

The fact that Richard is a journalist is otherwise intended to contextualize the factual, syncopated narrative style. There are echoes of the "hard-boiled" Hemingway style in this exchange between Hugo and Richard: " 'It sounds to me sometimes as if you've almost seen too much of the world.' 'And it sounds to me, Hugo, like you've seen too little'"(98) . And it is Jake Barnes's distinct voice taking leave of his café terrace friends that we hear when Richard thinks about doing the same in Havana: "Pretty soon, we were getting carried away, and I figured we might as well be making tracks" (105).

The use of a first-person narrator who is struggling with a guilty conscience, if not a wound of a sort --and whose words are therefore tainted with unreliability -- suggests a further association between Jake Barnes and Richard. His marriage to Diane has failed, yet he is not divorced, a choice he makes largely out of self-interest: it keeps him free of commitment (18). Jake Barnes knows of his sexual impotency yet he plays at love with Brett Ashley for what seems to amount to self-interest or a form of escapism. Richard's idea of freedom relates to the lack of emotional commitment. There is, then, a direct connection between the absent wife (Diane) and the absent lover (Lourdes in the end). Richard is the catalyst for escape in the context of his relationship with both women.

In more ways than one, the novel is deceptive in its choice of characterization, its use of obliqueness and understatement in narration, in the person of the narrator and in the use of dialogue, oral language, whence rests the issue of the narrator's reliability and the meaning of the story, as Conrad's Marlow says (*Heart of Darkness* 30). Where *Cuba and the Night* appears to fail as a novel much too grounded in the factually-based world of a photo-journalist, and in the sociological realities of contemporary Cuba, the reverse is true when José's father's cautionary words, as to what lies beneath the "mask" of picture-taking (190), are kept in mind. The book succeeds as a reflexive juxtaposition of the opposites of what is seen and unseen in photography for character development.

Looked at historically,*Cuba and the Night* is about Cuba of the "special period" of the early nineties when restrictions stemming from the breakup of the Soviet Union, Cuba's mentor State, led to food rationing and shortage, and the distinct prospect of economic collapse. As Elisa Facio demonstrates in her informative article ("Jineterismo During the Special Period"), the turning to tourism in search of foreign currency and a revival of prostitution were primary outlets for the State and for individuals, respectively, especially for young women who became sex workers in order to survive along with their families:

Jineteras are seeking power in the new tourist marketplace, the power of access to consumer goods and otherwise unobtainable amusements and diversions that are associated with the privileges of tourists and foreign businessmen. Some of the important differences between present-day *jineterismo* and pre-revolutionary prostitution are in the type of clients, educational access, family and social reactions, and levels of self-esteem. These changes are linked to the rapid development of tourism and increased opportunity for contact with foreign men.
Prostitution's customers used to be primarily Cuban men; today's clients are tourists from all over the world. (*Global Development Studies*)

The social context of that era is broadened in *Cuba and the Night* in Richard whose travels range from post-Vietnam Asia to postcolonial Africa and post-Castro South America to include Cuba as another example of a country which in his experience is merely one part of the world that has long lost its innocence (along with his). It is a world made of unrest, turmoil and destabilization in one form or another. What he finds in Cuba is personified by a number of individuals who are all hustlers that he has encountered the world over, hunkering for the fast buck.

He grows close to Lourdes who represents the impossibility of distinguishing the good from the bad in a world and a particular society that have been prostituted by History. Richard says:

The biggest shortage of all, I always thought, was of a future; the government mass-producing images of the past, while people kept their eyes firmly focused on the present....

Sometimes, in Cuba, it was like when you repeat the same word over and over till it stops making any sense....

Living in Havana in those days was like living with some medieval depiction of God: the guy was everywhere present and nowhere visible....

What --in Fidel's name-- was going on? (132-133)

* * *

In the Waste Land seen in Cuba by a Tiresias-like narrator, the love affair between Richard and Lourdes is described in purely sexual terms involving encounters on the streets, in bars and dance halls, where lust grows in proportion to frustrations and fears, and final gratification in dark farmhouses, alleyways, dingy rooms, taxis and rooftops --always with an ear open for the police and the fear of incarceration ("Everyone was looking at everyone else as if they were all targets or spies," 8; "The street was safer," 34). Bodies are focused upon because they are the determinants of perception in a world made of fondling, groping and grasping the unseen flesh living in the shadow of the State:

Then she was touching me on the leg, and her eyes were blazing as she talked. "Do you know what it is like, Richard, to live in a shadow? Everywhere I walk, there is the shadow of *El Lider*. He is everywhere I turn. His face is in the next room, and his eyes are watching through the window, and his voice is on the television in the neighbor's house, and his words are on the radio, and in *Granma*. He is everywhere: there is no room left for me. Except in the shadows." (117)

The hypocrisy of the State is particularly emphasized in Lourdes's repeated warnings to Richard of the penalties she faces if found in his company. Their love affair unfolds from one subterfuge to the next, and peaks in an idyllic stay at a Varadero resort (reserved by the State exclusively for tourists) as they pretend to be man and wife. It similarly flounders on subterfuge when Richard enlists Hugo's assistance to fool the authorities into letting Lourdes leave for England whence Richard will take her to America. The ruse boomerangs. Richard's hypocritical behavior with Caridad leads to Lourdes's choice to stay with Hugo in England.

Hypocrisy or failure in moral cogency and transparency practiced by the State and individuals seems to spill over in potential failure in aesthetic cogency and transparency in *Cuba and the Night*. Iyer's novel is occasionally clumsy in narrative structure; particularly evidenced in the use of letter-writing (for ex. 80-99) as a device for plot and character development. Derived from Cristina Garcia's *Dreaming in Cuban*, this device is here void of the integral legitimacy that validated Celia's character and Pilar's role as the artist figure. The dialogues are flat and clichéd and do not consistently play off Richard's intended world weariness. Characters are often given to monologues that are cloying because of their obvious sociological intent (Lourdes and José's father's recriminations about social inequities, 116-117; 186-190); they suggest the writer's incapacity to establish imaginative distance from events. The narrator is given to smart-alecky one-liners as if he were a stand-up comedian: "The Empire never died; it just got privatized" (95); "...it makes you think love is just war conducted by other means" (97); "Who was that guy I saw you with? That was no guy; that was my life" (98). Would-be profundities end up as clichés, "Coming to her was like coming home" (136); and stretching for effect results in bathos, "...somewhere, on the rocks, a woman sobbing and sobbing and sobbing" (34).

Style is at times flatly pedestrian ("I'm not thinking of the future; my job involves catching the moment," 94) when attention is not diverted by content focused on sexual acrobatics that are as tiresome as tedious (135-136; 139; 141; 146-147). To be sure, there is irony intended in juxtaposing the manic sexual and political activities ("Sex appeal and political irony all in the same pretty frame,"

23). But imagery is all too often caricatural in attempts at representing a world order in disarray by listing place names and events the world-weary journalist has experienced. The narrator then takes on the role of a ventriloquist bent on echoing the Indian-American writer Bharati Mukherjee's own ventriloquism in works mixing Asia, America and the Caribbean. Nationals of all those varied places uniformly speak the American tongue ("...like a suburb in Peru after twenty years of Burmese rule," 26).

Iyer's characters start off as cardboard figures, be it Lourdes as the prostitute-with-a-heart-of-gold; Richard, as the world-weary anti-hero straight from the fiction of Graham Greene (there are two references to *Our Man in Havana* [7, 216] as if the writer were unsure of the reader's ability to decode the character's typology); Hugo, Richard's surrogate friend, as the Somerset Maugham (20) type of Brit in the tropics; José, the go-between, as Defoe's Man Friday to Richard's Crusoe; and assorted hard-boiled journalists, like Mike Alvarez, of the Hemingway school.

* * *

Iyer deliberately risks having his book dismissed as superficial and derivative were it not for his consummate weaving of the tropical travel narrative with a modernist perspective that can be traced to his clear awareness of the precepts of some of its chief architects: Pound's understanding of the image, meshed with Cartier-Bresson's definition of photography; and Eliot's concept of myth underlying his use of the Waste Land tropism. *Cuba and the Night*'s representation of Havana as a den of rampant loveless sex and empty moral values is then raised to an aesthetic, modernist level.

Cuba and the Night subtly avoids disaster because it is a revisitation of literary modernism from a tropical angle. The representation of Havana as Eliot's London in the tropics brilliantly succeeds, starting with the predominant nighttime setting (*The Waste Land*'s "violet hour," III, 220) that opens the book (the Carnival evening, 4) and Richard, a Tiresias-like all-seeing --and blind-- first-person narrator, who sees himself as "the young man carbuncular" (III,220) whose relationship with Lourdes replicates the "young man's" bodily needs with the typist (*Ibid.*) reached for in so many "stairs unlit" (*Ibid.*) paralleled by dark corridors, alleys and staircases in the novel. It also succeeds when Pound's definition of the image is kept in mind as Richard's freezing of intellectual and emotional tenor in an "instant of time" in his picture-taking (the photos of Caridad) brings about his downfall.

In carnivalesque fashion, the text convincingly disguises Richard as a modernist artist figure who is morally defined by his use of the camera: "People tell lies, images never do" (19). The camera symbolizes the crux of his character, a point substantiated by José's father's admonition on adhering to surfaces (190), when Richard, speaking to Hugo, relativizes the truth of picture-taking and unconsciously parodies Pound: "It's not the whole truth, maybe, but it's true at that moment" (191).

A revised look at the text as an artistic whole reveals how the narrative dwells on surfaces for the purpose of contrasting the apparent simplicity of scenes and what in fact is hidden: the complicity of aberrations in behaviors, motives and characters brought on by the State's repressive policies, or, in a broader sense, the war-torn world that has shaped Richard's outlook. Thus the copious Havana place names strewn from the start in the narrative of well-known hotels like the Nacional, St. John's, Inglaterra, Capri, Habana Libre, Sevilla, Colina, Plaza, etc. correlate with the inventory of Richard's life that Havana represents. The narrator's worldwide experiences are localized and objectified in the hotels he patronizes; some of which were built by American mobsters and gangsters preceding the revolutionary years, and their legacy of lawlessness ironically carries on in carnival form which in effect subverts the prescriptions of the established revolutionary order.

Richard joins the people's carnivalesque lifestyle as soon as he steps out of the gangster-era hotels and explores the numerous streets and avenues of Central and Old Havana --La Rampa, Obispo, O'Reilly, Prado, Malecón, Presidente-- and parks like Parqueo Central and Coppelia. They are the "living rooms" of the people. There, a form of freedom is possible because spies and informers can be detected --even as they hide in bushes-- and the people can talk freely. The links between the hotels, streets, avenues and the parks are the bars, dance halls and hustlers (*jineteros* and *jineteras)*, the underground world of ordinary individuals eking a living from prostitution and other forms of illicit trading. (Richard meets José on La Rampa who introduces him to Lourdes, in Old Havana). The Malecón boulevard on the Bay of Havana designed for automobile traffic is actually the predominant route for trafficking in the sex trade.

The overall picture is one of decay, decrepitude, despair and disillusionment with the Revolution. And Richard finds in that picture a mirror of his own worldwide experiences. A whole nation has been turned into whores, stool pigeons and spies (8; 34). José Martí, claimed as the founder of modern Cuba, is frequently alluded to in the novel; he opens (25) and closes (234) the narrative, just as his presence covers the book's title taken from one of his poems: "Two fatherlands I have: Cuba and the Night" (25). The Martí reference is resonant: on the one hand, it means, as one character says, the distance the nation has fallen from the height of Martí's discourse of reconciliation and togetherness (63); and, further, the title begs for deconstruction --meaning whether there can now be a distinction between Cuba and the (endless) night it has fallen into.

Just as Richard learns the meaning of the verse line, "Cuba and the Night," from José, and appropriates it for his narrative, it also marks his demise in the end when the last picture in the book is figuratively taken in England. And it is that of an Anglicized (by clothing and skin tone) Lourdes leaning to pick up a book which Richard identifies as being Martí's. The novel closes as it began, at night; from an actual time marker to a metaphor for loss. If Eliot's *The Waste Land* was a meditation on the loss of value in the modern, urban world, *Cuba and the Night* is a dirge for a lost nation symbolized by Lourdes turned into an English matron, about to read Martí (who lived half of his life in exile) from abroad.

* * *

In accounting for the failure of the revolutionary State, Iyer's narrator makes his own comments, gives voice to obvious dissidents --even at the risk of repeated intrusive sociological editorializing. But where the text is successful is in the depiction of the *jinesterismo* world of hustlers and pimps who see the foreign visitor as a "prize specimen" (46), a "ticket out" (47) of the country. Deception becomes the norm in the struggle for life. Even Richard, who thinks he is fond of Lourdes, says: "...and I remembered why I liked her. I never could tell how much she meant what she was saying" (48).

The city's underground life is pictured with sound, and the focus is the practice of illicit trading matched by unrequited desires. Iyer's forte as a travel writer thrives; his eye for detail, his ear for sound, and his capacity to immerse himself into the foreignness of place --because each place is a mirror for the other-- are remarkable. Havana, as he says, has never been such a feast. It is steamy, in-your-face, aggressive, sexy, wild, crazy, an assault on the senses unto itself. The opening paragraph sets the tone and tempo:

I think I'll always remember the first time I saw him, in the bar of the old Nacional, on one of those messy Carnival evenings in July, the temperature about 120, with the blare of the floats and the trumpets carrying across the lawns, and the dancing young boys on the Malecón jiving over overflowing cups of beer, and the whole city kind of strutting its stuff and shimmying in the tropical night. (3)

Doubtless such a representation for a narrator who constantly plays with words accentuates the ironic symbolism of Lourdes's name, as the goal of a pilgrimage meant to heal the sick, the maimed and the disabled. Richard is the journalist disabled by the world he has experienced who, in the end, remains uncured because he has misunderstood and bartered Lourdes's real value in a bogus marriage. The good escapes him, and he bears responsibility for the failure of vision. (The photos he takes of Caridad, following his tryst with her during Lourdes's absence, are precisely the single item Lourdes invokes in her final letter to justify the end of their relationship.)

Beyond history and sociology, the book turns on vision put to good or false use, not unlike the dilemma faced by Walcott's narrator in *Omeros*. Though it borders on a leap of faith to see Richard as an artist figure in the company of Garcia's Pilar, Hemingway's Santiago or Walcott's narrator, it does not amount to a misreading of Iyer's novel to argue for its conscious adaptation of the Hemingwayesque iceberg technique. The adherence to surface, as the facts of

History, or the pictures of its results in contemporary Cuba, stand for a form of objectification wherein the real meaning of the novel lies in what is implied by the depiction of loveless sex as an entanglement of bodies. The chaotic urban landscape of T.S. Eliot's *The Waste Land* is thus revisited, transposed to the tropics. As well, the words seen as pictures call for their alignment with Pound's famous definition, as instants of time freezing an emotion and an idea all at once.

The influence of all three modernists --Hemingway, Eliot and Pound-- can be detected in the symbolism of the pictures found by Lourdes of Caridad in the same room, possibly same bed, and in the same hotel she and Richard shared in Varadero: they represent the tip of the iceberg of the overall incompatibility of emotion and reason in a Waste Land where both are corrupted.

* * *

A true and accurate reading of Iyer's book lies, then, in the deconstruction of the narrative, the act of seeing beyond the surface of the picture or the "mask," as one character puts it. The mask is the surface of contemporary urban Cuba, it is the official language of the State and the failed Revolution. It is a lie known by all those who have no alternative but to resort to the wearing of a mask, since the State itself sets the pace. In the end, the central moral issue is neither the prostitute, the petty hustler or the ordinary individual who panders for anything (the tourist dollar, the expected "gifts" from abroad from relatives or friends who have escaped and who are no longer heard from). It is neither Lourdes, nor Richard, with his failed vision, or even Hugo or José, the go-betweens who go where the wind blows.

The real issue is the existence of a Waste Land marked by the absence of an organic culture rooted in a regenerative mythology. Telling in that regard is the role played by the central myth in Cuban culture of the Virgen de la Caridad del Cobre (addressed by Garcia and Hemingway in their own works). Her shrine is visited by Lourdes and Richard in El Cobre on the eve of her wedding with Hugo. The description focuses on Lourdes behaving like numerous pilgrims: "...she'd brought a ring, she said, to give to the Virgin, to bring good luck to her marriage" (196). Her act of propitiation is critically and soundly assessed by Richard as useless when he divests himself of his camera: "There was something too much about the room, so I put away my camera and just looked at all the *heaped* and abandoned hopes of Cuba laid before its patron saint. ... then I got tired of waiting and went outside, into the sun" (197; italics added). Echoing Eliot's *Waste Land*'s "heap of broken images" (I,22), there is no virtue and no longer room for faith. Cuba, for Iyer, is another contemporary signpost for entropy, disorder and chaos in a fallen world: "It was like all the rooms in Cuba combined in one, all the private altars and glass cases pooled to make some communal appeal" (*Ibid.*).

Such a deep vision of the land is structured by three forms of agency: the narrative as a journalistic or phenomenological reportage, the specific form of the reportage by means of pictures, and the carnivalesque display of these pictures. The language's succinctness and dryness is a trope for the barrenness of the Waste Land setting. The starkness of the pictures taken means to represent life as is, in accordance with Henri Cartier-Bresson's definition of the relationship between "life" and photography. Finally, the carnival motif underlies disguise, subterfuge, deceit that escape anyone's control, including the narrator's: "Even the simplest things were complex here" (55).

Chapter Seven
Carnival in Greeneland: Greene's *Our Man in Havana*

To look at Graham Greene's *Our Man in Havana*, published one year before the Revolution, is to flash back to an earlier Cuba seen in a rearview mirror. And what is seen is the advent of a society's carnivalesque form dramatized in deceptively dour fashion, yet symbolic of dissent, by Iyer. Given the prescience characteristic of Greene's imaginative vision of the relationship between setting and self conveying the universality of the human condition, Pico Iyer could not but pay homage to his predecessor by referring to him by name and have a character tell of the circumstances of the writing of *Our Man in Havana* "on the veranda of the Nacional" (7) --while his own central character is introduced in the bar of the same hotel-- at the very outset of *Cuba and the Night* (3).

It is clear that Greene's shadow looms large over Iyer's novel. First, it is Iyer's way of indicating that in the genealogy of travel writing mixed with fiction he recognizes Greene as his mentor. He shares Greene's view of the human condition as carnivalesque; i.e. individuals covering up their real selves in a world deemed to be absurd and void of values ("Reality in our century is not something to be faced," 10). As in *Cuba and the Night*, the carnival motif is a unifying thread in *Our Man in Havana*.

Greene's central characters are likely to be world weary, disillusioned, at "the end of their rope," so to speak. They have traveled the world over and witnessed how in places far apart from each other, the apartness of individuals in relationships and moral values parallels the state of modernity seemingly abandoned by the gods and left to fend for itself in a Waste Land. Thus we have the Consul in *The Quiet American*, the "whisky priest" in *The Power and the Glory*, Dr. Magiot in *The Comedians*, Querry in *A Burnt-Out Case*, Scobie in *The*

Heart of the Matter, all of whom shaped in the mold of the Greenean anti-hero out of which evolves Pico Iyer's Richard.

As well, the typical use of somewhat exotic settings in Greene ranging from Vietnam to Africa, and from Central America to the Caribbean, as a way of stressing the universality of the human condition, is liberally appropriated by Iyer for the depiction of Richard as a world-traveled photo-journalist. Just as Greene made use of Vietnam (*The Quiet American)*, Mexico (*The Power and the Glory)*, West Africa (*The Heart of the Matter*; *A Burnt-Out Case)*, Haiti (*The Comedians*) and other places, Iyer makes a similar inventory of the world to bring out the character of Richard.

Greene's comic worldview, meant to backdrop the tragic condition of individuals, is foregrounded in the rule of disguise, mistaken identity, subterfuge and subversion displayed by characters such as Petit Pierre in *The Comedians*, Deo Gratias, in *A Burnt-Out Case,* the *mestizo* in *The Power and the Glory.* It is not unnoticed by Iyer in his portrayal of Hugo, the comic foil for Richard who eventually settles with the world as is, rather than engage in the kind of blind pursuit where the Greene and Iyer anti-hero fails.

Finally, Greene's shadow is explained by Iyer's choice of subject for his first novel: Cuba. Perhaps more than writers like Hemingway and Garcia, Greene charted the course for the representation of Cuba in a world context (that of the Cold War) that Iyer builds on by setting his own view of Cuba in the post-Vietnam period that closely followed the Cold War. Greene used Cuba of the pre-Revolution era as a blank sheet that he filled by positioning the country as a prey to predators from the East and the West that make use of it for their own interests. He draws individuals that are largely comic characters who find themselves playing the roles of pawns in a game (Wormold gets the better of Captain Segura playing checkers, 191-196), stage comedy or carnival where the only victor is the clown: "The cruel come and go like cities and thrones, leaving their ruins behind them. They had no permanence... But the clown...was permanent, for his act never changed. That was the way to live; the clown was unaffected by the vagaries of public men and the enormous discoveries of the great" (32).

Iyer's time period reverses the stress from comic to tragic. Greene supplied the necessary terms for the dialectic of good and evil that both writers share. A reading of *Our Man in Havana* through the lens of literary appropriation germane to Iyer's novel yields, then, an enhanced appreciation of Greene's novel.

* * *

A close analysis of *Our Man in Havana* is revealing not only of many features that are passed on to *Cuba and the Night*, but of the use and function of the pre-revolutionary Cuba portrayed by Greene.

I will be discussing the salient features that allow for the continued relevance of *Our Man in Havana* to present-day Cuba: the carnivalesque picture related to the postwar as a basis for the comic use of disguise and mistaken identity; the characterization of James Wormold, Dr. Hasselbacher, Captain Segura and others; the depiction of the city and the sex trade in bars, hotels, streets, whorehouses, etc.; the cryptic use of language; and the significance of the Greenean look.

To start in reverse chronology, Greene's gaze is universally consistent. Turned on Cuba, it focuses on the desultory life of Wormold, a British expatriate vacuum cleaner salesman in Havana whose closest friend is Hasselbacher, a retired German doctor. Both define their lives by their morning ritual at the Wonder Bar, their relationship with the landscape of familiar streets and districts (Lamparilla, Obispo, O'Reilly, Virtudes, Belgica, Paseo, Vedado), nightclubs and bars (Tropicana, Havana Club, Floridita, the defunct Shangai Theatre), hotels (Seville-Biltmore, Nacional, Inglaterra), and their sighting of Cubans from a distance as characters on a stage that includes the sex trade ("...he embarked on the great Havana subject; the sexual exchange was not only the chief commerce of the city, but the whole *raison d'être* of a man's life. One sold sex or one bought it -- immaterial which, but it was never given away," 56). Both are displaced from their observation posts by the arrival of an agent from the British Secret Service who enlists Wormold in a spy scheme he goes along with to support his daughter's taste for horseback riding.

Wormold's activities as a spy are limited to inventing and performing his role as he goes along. He is mentored by Dr. Hasselbacher:

" 'The other day I was offered money.'
'Yes?'
'To get information.'
'What sort of information?'
'Secret information.' ...
'If it is secret enough, you alone know it. All you need is a little imagination, Mr. Wormold.
'They want me to recruit agents. How does one recruit an agent, Hasselbacher?'
'You could invent them too, Mr. Wormold.'
'You sound as though you had experience.' " (57-58)

Like a fiction writer, Wormold makes up stories of sites and informers (he is told by Beatrice: "You talk like a novelist," 108). His fiction-making turns against him as his stories are picked up and trusted by an opposite party that includes Dr. Hasselbacher's German past and results in his murder while Wormold himself is the target for assassination by poison which he eludes. If Hasselbacher's comic role is limited to his accent and accouterment, Wormold's is at the heart of the novel. He is the bumbling innocent-type recurrent in Greene's fiction whose presence away from home (he has been living in Havana for fifteen years) is as much to establish distance from an absent wife as to relate to a no man's land void of obligations and responsibilities other than the selling of vacuum cleaners. It is from that presumed safe world he finds himself removed and turned into a clown whose pratfalls with the Cuban police (his foil is a Captain named Segura, "the Red Vulture," 36), the British Secret Service (his initial handler Hawthorne is soon replaced by a secretary, Beatrice, who mirrors his own innocence), the European Traders' Association (at a luncheon at the Nacional that is a masterpiece of carnivalesque comedy where no one is what he appears to be as Wormold proceeds to avoid drinking a deadly poison, 169-178) cumulate with his recall to London to receive the Order of the British Empire for brilliantly performing in His Majesty's service!

Obviously, Greene wrote a satirical novel using a Cuban setting for dramatic effect better to debunk what he believed --in numerous novels-- to be the recurrent stupidity, denseness and pomposity of officialdom (especially emphasized in the dénouement, when Wormold is awarded the O.B.E., 213-217). People do die in *Our Man in Havana* (Hasselbacher, Raúl, Carter), and so does a dog named "Max," the headwaiter's, which drinks the poison intended for Wormold. People are beaten up (Wormold in Santiago, 64-65; and Captain Segura's philosophy of torture is eloquently described, 150-151). And there are rumors of "the usual rebels" (63) in Oriente province (Fidel Castro and his cohorts who remain nameless), notwithstanding the tension of the Cold War making of Cuba a site for a dubious battle between shadowy characters, but one that foreshadows the missile crisis of 1962. Says Segura: "'Of course, we are only a small country, but we lie very close to the American coast. And we point at your own Jamaica base. If a country is surrounded, as Russia is, it will try to punch a hole through from inside" (150).

Wormold's gaze never fixes a Cuban other than Captain Segura. Segura's unsavory reputation ("He specializes in torture and mutilation," says Hasselbacher, 36) is sufficient for the official violence he represents (" 'Torture?' says Wormold. 'There's nothing here,' replies Hasselbacher," *Ibid.*). It is brought out in the scene at the Tropicana when Segura's importuning of Wormold's daughter is dealt with by Beatrice who splashes him with soda water (86). Segura's threatened revenge (which, in fact never materializes) is on a par with his sinister character as he takes leave of Beatrice: " 'If you have any trouble with your permit,' he said ambiguously, 'you must come to me' " (87). The function of such a scene anticipates the one in Santiago when Wormold is taken into custody and lies his way out, as well as the luncheon scene. Similarly, Segura's sexual design on Wormold's daughter is carefully hinted at; and even Milly's language is teasing in that regard, testing her father's reaction (21, 43, 84-85). Altogether, these scenes suggest the role assigned to violence and villainy as real, but their being commonplace, and universal, reduce their meaningfulness here to caricatures and grotesqueries.

Captain Segura's lusting for Milly is grotesque and laughable, but so is the agent sent to kill Wormold (who kills Hasselbacher by default), Carter, whose dysfunctionality is satirized when he is taken to a whorehouse (201). Whores, pimps and assorted riff-raff pollute the Havana air sniffed from a distance by Wormold. They represent figures of decadence of a postwar world which found its way to pre-revolutionary Cuba. If there is any redemption for such a world it is hinted at by the references to the rebels in the hills of Oriente province, but neither it nor they materialize, no more than the identity of the actual spies and counter-spies lurking in the shadows.

What redemption exists is contained in the anti-heroic character of the bumbling naïf Wormold represents (whose name indicates his lowly significance akin to Arthur Miller's naming of Loman in his 1949 play, *Death of a Salesman*). His name is a pun: "old-as-worm." Hasselbacher's name also suggests a comment on anomie: as a "backer" of "hassle." Like so many Greene characters (the Consul in *The Quiet American*, Querry, in *A Burnt-Out Case*), Wormold is the innocent, ordinary individual whose very ordinariness is designed to contrast with the degraded, unregenerated world that preys on him. He is brought out of his insignificance by agents of such a world singled out by the Home Office and his "handler," Hawthorne, who is himself manipulated by his supervisor, The Chief, who is never named and is, in turn, set up to "perform" for his Minister. It is a topsy-turvy carnivalesque world where everyone wears a mask that is not matched by the character beneath the mask. The Chief is a ruler whose rule rests on nothingness, only pretense.

Thus, Cuba is the microcosm of a larger world Wormold tried to flee. His significance is that he is the only one who makes the reconciliation between wearing the mask of a lowly vacuum cleaner salesman and the one that he easily substitutes as a spy. He is an actor who knows his role in a story whose relationship with life is fiction. A Shakespearean undertone obviously underlies his characterization (Shakespeare is twice alluded to in the book: *A Misummer's Night Dream*, 83-84; and *Macbeth*, 115). Life being a stage for him, he triumphs in the end as a Shakespearean clown who survives because he knows of the "permanence" of the stage in contrast with the delusion of "public men" engaged in the practice of power. [Greene gives a revealing description of his seeing Fidel Castro giving a speech in 1966:

> Knowing little Spanish I observed his physical performance rather than listened to his speech. I could have divided it like a play into acts: in the first act he was a grave formidable figure, almost motionless at the podium, the word *consciencia* chimed in his sentences. Then suddenly all changed to comedy and farce, as he imitated the ignorant member of a political *cadre*, *"No sé, No sé." Collected Essays* 304.]

* * *

Wormold's redeeming value is like the priest's in *The Power and the Glory*, Querry's in *A Burnt-Out Case*, Scobie's in *The Heart of the Matter*: it lies in his anti-heroism, his flawed embodiment of meekness.

Telling of Wormold's "ordinariness" is his use of language in dead-pan, cryptic form. Talking to his daughter Milly, Beatrice, Hasselbacher or Segura, he always seems to be one step behind the other's facility with language. He appears as unsure of his daughter who *knows* Segura before he does (" 'Who's Captain Segura, Milly?' 'The head police officer in Vedado.' 'Where on earth did you meet him?' 'Oh, he often gives me a lift to Lamparilla in his car.,' " 21). Hasselbacher subsequently informs him of Captain Segura's reputation: " 'Who's the Red Vulture?' 'Captain Segura, of course,' Dr. Hasselbacher said. 'What a sheltered life you lead.' " 36). Milly *knows* what is behind the story of Segura taking her out to her riding lessons: "He said, 'You aren't in love, are you, with this Captain Segura?' Two tears chased each other with a kind of elegance round the curve of a cheek-bone and glittered like the harness on the wall; they were part of her equipment too" (21).

Wormold is in the dark and can only mutter a lame prescription that Milly not marry Segura " 'You must drop him, Milly' 'I shall --slowly...' " (43). His exchanges with Segura, on the other hand, are echoes of Hawthorne's with his boss, The Chief: essentially comic interludes where the man of power controls discourse because of what he represents, not really for what he actually says. Segura's speech is replete with undertones of sexual masculine power (what he might do to Beatrice, Milly, Teresa, etc.), against which Wormold pits his own language in the game of Checkers, shouting out the pawns as he overcomes Segura. (It is important to note how it is his mastery of a game, like his mastery of acting as a metaphor, that provides him with a reliable non-verbal language.) Talking with Hasselbacher, he is the drinking companion who from the start is behind in the use of language when Hasselbacher refers to a limping passer-by (7) as someone who looks like him. Wormold reflects rather on the triviality of never being called by his first name by Hasselbacher (whom he never addresses on that basis either, but he does not see the irony). He falls in love with Beatrice but he neither uses the word nor owns up to the emotion because of his knowledge of the Waste Land. Beatrice gets to know him and settles for a future which is envisaged in the closing lines of the book: "... and she realized the chief problem of their future --that he would never be quite mad enough" (220).

Beyond individual characterization, it is the author or his persona that ultimately controls the novel. Greene delights in word plays, as already seen in the names given to his two central characters. The short sentences in dialogues are designed to suggest how the characters are performing on a stage. He has fun with sounds, drawing attention to Hasselbacher and Carter's German accent (singling out the "stammered aspirate,"176), and Lopez's inability to pronounce Wormold's name properly ("Vormell...Ommel...Vormole...Venell...Vommold," 55-56). He is the master of the pithy line: " 'Wonderful,' Wormold said. It was his invariable answer, but he meant it" (8). And irony is invested in language that comments on the author's sense of his craft matching Wormold's self-understanding of the world-as-a-stage:

"'But Raúl --he didn't even exist. You advised me to lie and I lied. They were nothing but inventions, Hasselbacher.'
'And Cienfuegos? Are you telling me he didn't exist either?'
'He was different. I invented Raúl.'
'Then you invented him too well, Mr. Wormold. There's a whole file on him now.'
'He was no more real than a character in a novel.'
'Are they always invented? I don't know how a novelist works, Mr. Wormold. I have never known one before you.' " (141)

* * *

All in all, Greene's gaze on his central character, Wormold, is reflected in the latter's role in a no man's land of a country whose absurd trade (selling vacuum cleaners for use indoors in a tropical land where life is lived mainly outdoors, witness the bar hopping, hotels and other landmarks of Havana where the action unfolds) is mirrored by the absurd role he is asked to take (spying), and that he absurdly performs by resorting to myth-making. Early on, he is told by his mentor, Hasselbacher, to take his inspiration from Sir James Frazer's research on myth: "And there is something about a secret which makes people believe... perhaps a relic of magic. Have you read Sir James Frazer?" (58). That Sir James Frazer's *The Golden Bough* was the source for T. S.Eliot's *The Waste Land* adds to the universal resonance of a sardonic view of modernity shared by Greene, Eliot and Iyer. Cuba or Havana is the name given to a place which is, in fact, a mask for human folly.

Greene sees Cuba as mirroring the human condition. He satirizes a world of bad actors, of "public men" in England as well as Cuba (be they Hawthorne, The Chief, Segura or "the usual rebels"). He focuses on one individual as an Everyman whose behavior is modeled on a world seen as a stage where the comic character of the clown is the one remaining hero. His gaze is sweeping, seeing society as a sterile and destructive Cold War inhabited by shadowy characters from shadowy countries whose first allegiance should be to something other than "country."

In Beatrice's closing words (whose name resonates with her Dantesque counterpart's role as a redemptive guide): "I can't believe in anything bigger than a home, or anything vaguer than a human being" (217). Which is what *Our Man in Havana* is all about when one thinks of Hasselbacher and Wormold's expatriates' gaze matching that of Garcia's Pilar, Constancia and Reina, Hemingway's Santiago, Walcott's narrator, Iyer's Richard, and even Desnoes's nameless narrator. They are all in the end looking for a home of their own believing.

Chapter Eight

The Unreliable Narrator's Gaze: Desnoes's *Inconsolable Memories*

Edmundo Desnoes's *Inconsolable Memories* is also about a salesman in Havana who used to sell Simmons furniture until his store was nationalized by the revolutionary government. He is lower than Greene's Wormold on the human scale, though his epithet in Spanish, *gusano* (86), also means "worm." While Greene's novel was set a year before the advent of the Revolution, Desnoes's picks up where the former leaves off. It is the first-person monologue of an alienated middle-class Cuban living in Havana up to the 1962 missile crisis. The novel opens with his just having seen his parents and his estranged wife off to exile in the U.S.

The nameless narrator chooses to stay behind and he tells his story in diary form, using a voice strongly resonant of Albert Camus' Meursault in *L'Etranger* (1957). Camus is in fact mentioned by Desnoes in an interview in *La Jiribilla*: "Eso me desgarró, como en el caso de Camus, salvando la distancia. Mantener una posición clara y no simplemente tomar partido, creo que es esencial" ("Thus I found myself split, like Camus, keeping a safe distance. Maintaining a clear position and not simply take sides: I think this is essential." *My translation*).The narrator's story is of his disenfranchisement from the new regime ("The Revolutionary government doesn't know what kind of mess it's got itself into," 19) and the middle class of his upbringing (" I can't think of the Cuban bourgeoisie without foaming at the mouth," 29).

The story behind Desnoes's novel is peculiar. It was originally published in Cuba in 1965, and in Argentina in 1968. Translated into English by the author, it appeared in revised form in the U.S. (the Hemingway sequence was added and the missile crisis scene expanded) in 1967 and England, the following year. The author, who spent some ten years in the U.S. before returning to his native island in 1960 worked in the State publishing industry, helped to found the Casa de las Américas (a cultural group best known now for its sponsoring of an annual literary competition and its editing of an eponymous magazine), and he edited or wrote for a number of literary magazines for close to two decades. He again left Cuba in 1981 for the U.S. Recent information, subsequent to his returning to Cuba as a visitor in early 2003, is his planning on dividing his time between the two countries.

Desnoes was apparently warmly received in 2003 by former friends and fellow writers (see *La Jiribilla*, an arts review published by Casa de las Américas), though some exiled writers had mixed feelings about his return. Belkis Cuza Malé, Heberto Padilla's widow, wrote in *La Nueva Cuba*:

Ahora Edmundo Desnoes está de nuevo en la Casa de las Américas. No importa que incluso la desillusion haya llevado a su directora a pegarse un tiro. El hijo pródigo ha regresado y lo hace con lágrimas en los ojos. Por primera vez siente que ha triunfado, que está en el sitio del que nunca debió salir. Alli están sus amigos de siempre, que lo tratan ahora con un respeto special....

¿Acosono sabe que precisamente ahora el país se hunde cada dia mas en el desconsuelo y la desperanza, gracias el tirano Fidel Castro; que la isla está llena de disidentes; que las cárceles albergan cadea día a más presos politicos; que la gente, hambrienta y tratando de sobrevivir, no está alli para aplaudiro? (*La Nueva Cuba*)

(Edmundo Desnoes is now back in Casa de las Américas. It is needless to recall the price he paid for disillusionment when he was its director. The prodigal son has returned with tears in his eyes. For once he feels recognized, that he is in a place that he should have never left. There are his old friends treating him with special respect....

Doesn't he know that precisely at the same moment the country is sinking each day into dejection and despair, thanks to the tyrant Fidel Castro; that the island is full of dissidents; that prisons are filled each day with political prisoners; that the people are hungry and trying to survive, and that they are not among those there to applaud him? *My translation*.)

The novel's subject, the uncommitted life of an alienated writer, is told in a contrapuntal discourse. It juxtaposes the "official line" (the Revolution's mixed with the counter-revolution's) and the narrator's subtextual discourse (his surface expression of alienation and discontent masking a contrasting, albeit carefully hidden, critique of the narrator's reliability) that facilitated its reception in revolutionary Cuba, no doubt with the assistance of Desnoes's literate friends at the Casa de las Américas. The figure of the anti-hero in a State that values revolutionary heroism comes off in spite of being tagged with the worst of epithets (*gusano*). He is obviously meant to be understood as a cautionary example of what the Revolution has no use for.

The Cuban setting appears at times to be accidental. The alienation, anomie and unease the nameless narrator shares with Sartre's Roquentin, Camus' Meursault and Greene's characters altogether would have been the same irrespective of countries.

The terms of his alienation are further specified in the figure of his friend Pablo who represents the bourgeoisie that has been displaced by the Revolution. Pablo flees the island once he reaches the limits of recriminations. Women appear as buoys. But starting with Laura, the narrator's estranged wife, they fail to rescue him. His wife is a female Pablo, a superficial moneygrubber who is remembered as loathsome by the narrator. He remembers Hanna who left for New York. His affair with a girl he meets on the street, Elena, turns sour and he escapes conviction on a morals charge when it is revealed in court that she was once arrested for prostitution. Finally, he has a sexual relationship with Noemi who is submissive and supportive like Emma, an older woman, but unlike the others who were not. Like the other women, Noemi fades away.

The narrator is further alienated as a writer who finds fault with his colleagues, like Eddy, who is a "sell-out": "...yesterday I saw him seated up on a dais smoking a cigar and pontificating about literature," 83). Even the venerable Alejo Carpentier is described in ambiguous terms ("...not interested in the jungle, or his novels about the grotesque repercussions of the French Revolution in the Caribbean," 79). The problem the narrator wrestles with is the adequacy of the literary sources that feed his imagination, inform his notion of standards and respect for language. On all three points he is European-bred, yet he lives in Cuba. The problem is how to reconcile his sense of "civilization" or "development" with what he repeatedly harps on as "underdevelopment," or what he sees as the backwardness of life in Cuba before and during the revolutionary years. He sums up by referring to the Cuban innate lack of responsibility and propensity to turn everything into a joke-- to the extent of wondering whether Castro does not belong to the general mold: "Cubans can't endure suffering too long without laughing. The sun, the tropics, irresponsibility.... Is Fidel that way too?" (53).

As a disenfranchised salesman, the narrator not only evokes his counterpart in *Our Man in Havana* but also Willy Loman in Arthur Miller's *Death of a Salesman*. He belongs to the typology of the Everyman living under a capitalist system that turns him into a cheap commodity, good only for temporary use and replaced as fast as a new gadget is on the market. Seen in that light, Desnoes's anti-heroic character, clearly designed as a tropical expression of European *angst*, is firmed up by his closeness to an American context that, in addition, includes his love-hate relationship with Hemingway (71; discussed later).

* * *

Beyond the ambiguous, political double-dealing of the design of the novel, its story line rests on a worldview of sterility and waste similar to Greene's and Iyer's. It is informed by postwar European existentialism in which one can easily denote overtones of Sartre's *La Nausée* (1938) and Camus' *L'Etranger* (1957). The title of the book is taken from a line spoken in a film that the narrator says marked his life, Alain Resnais' *Hiroshima, mon amour* (1958), when a character says "J'avais désiré avoir une inconsolable mémoire" (37) ("I yearned for an inconsolable memory." *My translation*). Repeated twice (52), that line signals how the novel is meant to fit in a postwar European literary and philosophical context it shares with *Our Man in Havana*. Its closeness to European literary sources is emphasized by the narrator's readings, literary allusions and travels and his constant negative comparisons with his native land characterized over and over as "underdeveloped" along with its citizens --especially his estranged wife, Laura, who ironically bears the name of Petrarch's muse better to emphasize her hopeless (for the narrator) middle-class materialist tastes and values: "All Laura wants is comfort and a touch of romanticism. I've seen the horse's ass: working to support her as if she had been born in New York or Paris (and bourgeois, as they say here these days) and not on this underdeveloped island" (14).

The narrator's repeated deprecations of his estranged wife --"taking trips to civilized countries, trying to make her refined, making all kinds of efforts to avoid getting caught up in the vicious circle of recriminations" (*Ibid.*)-- extend to his whole society and, ironically, includes him. There is a culture clash at the heart of the novel; and it is that of one man's understanding of what constitutes "civilization" and "underdevelopment" based on alienated cultural values he is seemingly unaware of sharing with the objects of his recriminations.

The kind of unconscious irony built in the character of the narrator is an indication of the subtlety Desnoes brings to his narrative which prevented it from being perceived as a rejection and critique of the Revolution. It explains to a certain extent why it saw publication in revolutionary Cuba. The problem, then, starts with an unreliable narrator, and how his unreliable point of view disqualifies the truth of what he says about the society. That is to say, his unreliability and moral shallowness are shared by each other character whose story he gets to tell. It includes, besides his estranged wife, his close friend Pablo, his literary colleague Eddy (identified as "Edmundo Desnoes," no less! "Once you were young and pure, Eddy, and look at yourself now, Edmundo Desnoes," 81). Eddy's novel that he criticizes intriguingly resembles the story the narrator is telling: "The plot is simply puerile: an uprooted Cuban (with existentialist frosting), after a frustrating affair with a mulatto maid and rejecting a wealthy American heiress, decides to integrate himself into Cuban life here" (77). But for the reference to an "American heiress," everything else in that quote applies to Desnoes's novel, even filling in what is actually left open in the end; i.e. "[integration] into Cuban life." The mirroring of narratives and of narrators echoes Conrad's practice in *Heart of Darkness*, but the model Desnoes acknowledges is Cervantes's *Don Quixote* and its use of doubles.

The narrator's unreliability is revealed as well in his account of his relationships with women. In addition to Laura, his descriptions of Elena, Hanna, Emma and Noemi add up to the sameness of his dissatisfaction with their surface appearances he lusts for and gratifies, only to end up with the sameness of malaise, unease and alienation.

* * *

Hemingway's legend comes in for an extended critical assessment contextualized by a visit the narrator pays to his house turned into a museum by the State. Though it is predicated on his unsupported opinion that Hemingway was "a second-rate artist" (82) --yet his own barren style of writing is typically Hemingway's-- his iconoclastic discourse is objectified by the construct of the house itself, its rooms and decorations and ruins. Not surprisingly, Elena, who is with him, mysteriously finds herself at the bottom of an empty pool on the property and frighteningly asks for help. The element of fear is meant to characterize the property and the dead owner as threatening or ghostlike. The sense of decay and otherworldliness the property exudes ties in with the concept of myth the text addresses (to be discussed later). On a primary level, that scene is consistent with the function of landscape throughout as an objective correlative for the narrator's inner state of despair and alienation.

In clever fashion, Desnoes sets up from the start his narrator's unreliability in the context of his gaze which is faulty. He is nearsighted and in need of glasses to gain a broader perspective ("I went to have a pair of glasses made so I could see clearly from a distance," 38). Not only his sight is in need of correction, but his hearing is also defective ("I went to see the picture again because I had missed some snatches of dialogue," 37). His whole body is giving up on him, maybe because of age and lack of exercise --he is developing a paunch-- or maybe it is simply genetics; he takes after his own father:

I'm growing old. It's devastating to see how your body crumbles from so much use, slips away out from under you. Now I'm obsessed with doing some exercise. Got too much of a paunch.... Looked at myself in the mirror and discovered with surprise that I was beginning to look like my father: I've got the same kind of stomach.... That really depressed me. When I sit down two inner tubes of fat encircle my waist. (38)

Maurice Merleau-Ponty's *Phenemenology of Perception* is the theoretical foundation for Desnoes's delineation of the narrator's body as a metaphor for the malaise and psychological despair that plague the narrator. If his words are unreliable, his body and other bodies tell the truth. Besides the women's that fail him, those of the counter-revolutionaries appear as grotesque. First there is Pablo: "The only intelligent thing Pablo ever had to say would end up degenerating into a discussion about stupid food" (39). He has Pablo's bodily bulk inferred in his own words: "Don't be foolish, I'm anything but fat. It's a question of my constitution, that's how I'm built. Besides, you don't have any idea of the troubles I go through. You don't know how I have to scheme to eat well, to nourish myself" (*Ibid.*). As a whole, the body is used as a metaphor to characterize the counter-revolutionaries' alienation: "If I still believed in or could even create any illusion about the counter-revolution, it's all over now; it's gone to hell. Nothing in their heads, no dignity, no backbone; the middle class here is like a meringue on the door of a school, as they say, yes, a meringue on the door of the revolution" (38).

The gaze can be corrected ("Got the glasses," 45). The body can be improved ("The body can be very grateful. In less than a week of exercises, I can already feel my muscles tightening. My stomach sticks out less," *Ibid.*). Sight and body do correlate like the paragraphs relating the two on the page just quoted. More significantly, it may be a way for the author to signal a shift from the narrator's bald unreliabilty to newly found reliability when his subsequent accounting is informed by clearsightedness, a move from myopia to a broader vision. Thus attention is called to the narrator's improved gaze: "I can see, it's true, with greater precision. Before everything was blurred, with fuzzy edges, like impressionist paintings, and now I can see everything with the transparent accuracy of an Ingres. Don't know which picture I like better. It's difficult, having to choose all the time!" (*Ibid.*).

It is that improved gaze that he shortly thereafter brings to bear on Hemingway's house (55) as he discreetly appropriates the myth of the American Dream and reverses it. If his parents, his wife, Hanna, and his friend Pablo are all tropical dreamers who set forth for the materialization of the Dream in the U.S., the text neatly draws attention to the living legend in Cuba of Ernest Hemingway as an embodiment of the blind reverence Cubans have for the American Dream. It is perpetuated in the museum the State has turned Hemingway's house into in San Francisco de Paula. For the narrator, it essentially stands for the perpetuation of American colonialism in its conquering form, leaving behind a colonized former servant who acts as tour guide.

The visit paid to the house is described at length (55-74); every room is described in detail as well as the property, notably the pool and the tower Hemingway's wife, Mary, had built for him. There is Hemingway's former domestic, René Villarreal ("You could see that Hemingway had molded him according to his needs, twisted him into shape, the faithful servant. The colonizer and Gunga Din," 64). His real name and function are confirmed by Norberto Fuentes in *Hemingway in Cuba*.

Fuentes includes an account of Villarreal's reaction to Desnoes's portrayal of him replicated in the film version of the book (*Memories of Underdevelopment*). He quotes Tomás Gutiérrez, the film director:

At one point, the off-screen voice of the main character accuses him of having been a "slave" to Hemingway.... " The man did not seem to understand that the film was a work of fiction," says Tomas Gutiérrez Alea, the director. "When the film was shown in the theaters, René got a gun and went looking for Edmundo and me. He wanted to kill us. " (38)

The guided tour includes some gauche Russian visitors insistently identified by their foul smell (55, 60, 68), next to the narrator and Elena. The deep symbolism of their visit is a revisitation of the notion of myth, American myth, applied to Cuba's identity. The narrator sums it up in a nutshell in the guide's subservient language, in his [the narrator's] observations on the furnishings and decoration, and his musings about the relationship between Hemingway and Cuba: "I thought that Cuba never really meant a fucking thing to Hemingway....Nowhere in the whole house was there anything Cuban, not even an Afro-Cuban witchcraft conversation piece or a painting. Nothing" (71-72).

The narrator raises the question of Cuba's identity up to the Revolution as a mere colony of the U.S. And he doubly insists on the unchanged nature of that relationship exemplified by Hemingway's former servant acting as guide, and by the presence of the Russian visitors, the would-be protectors of the new Cuban State who slavishly admire Hemingway: "They're desperate to catch up with the United States and become the Americans of the future, they admire Hemingway more than they admire Fidel, I bet you anything they have more respect for Hemingway than for Fidel" (58).

He corroborates Greene's representation of Cuba as fuel for the rivalry between the U.S. and the USSR. It exists for each major power's self-interest:

> Always the same. Emissaries of the great world power down visiting their colonies. The same fucking tourists. Humbler men than most Americans, true, and without any holdings in Cuba --but deep down their attitude is very much alike. Besides, what they can't take away in dollars they get out of us in propaganda....That's all they're good for, underdeveloped countries, good for fulfilling our instinctive drives, killing wild animals, fishing and basking in the sun. (56)

What is left unsaid is the Cuban State's participation in the maintenance of U.S. cultural colonialism in the iconization of its most famous foreign resident. The danger faced is symbolized by Elena's fall into the empty pool, Desnoes's adaptation of the Narcissus myth: "'Help, 'elp, 'elp!' Elena screamed from the bottom of the pool" (73). The narrator's questions as to how she got there are answered by Elena's "don't know" (74). The point is, of course, the unknowingness or blindness of Narcissus-like colonial imitation.

The extended visit to Hemingway's house may well be the part of the book that stands for the whole. It raises the narrative from a confessional, self-absorbed --at times tedious whine by a not particularly likeable character-- to a level of counter-discourse that questions the U.S. and USSR forms of subjugation Cuba is still a prey to. In that sense, the book is a sobering critique of the Revolution. It suggests, among other things, that the narrative is about self and collective identity, self-delusion and alienation. The narrator visiting Hemingway's house sees his own self-hate: "I have mixed feelings. I feel love and hate toward Hemingway; I admire him and at the same time he humiliates me. The same as my people; it's the same feeling I have when I think of Fidel, of the revolution.

Permanently split; I can't even agree with a part of myself" (71).

In the above passage, the narrator dramatically analyzes himself and provides a context for his self-deprecation and dour view of his society. He is as hard on himself, and on women, as he is on the Revolution. Yet he is not a Pablo; his stance is a Quixotic one, he is still inspired by an utopia whose materialization he does not see around him, but the opposite in the chronic food shortages, the lack of basic products, and the creeping bureaucracy. Don Quixote is mentioned by Desnoes in the *La Jiribilla* interview: "Toda la literatura, *Don Quijote*, *Hamlet*, está hecha con elementos de fracaso, es una ilusión vana pensar que vamos a triunfar siempre." ("All of literature, Don Quixote, Hamlet, is made of fractured fragments; it's a vain illusion to think that we are always going to win.")

* * *

Inconsolable Memories is a book that reflects the gaze of a disappointed lover who equates the shortcomings of the women in his life (who personify the land) with the dismal landscape he has chosen to inhabit. It is a frustrated lover's gaze who wanted more out of the dreamed body of Laura, Hanna, Elena, Emma and Noemi. To that extent it is a novel of desire, longing for something better than what the gaze perceives on the surface. An inner vision qualifies the appearance of things: it is other than unsympathetic to the land, the very opposite.

The novel closes with the threat of annihilation it shares with a central passage in Benítez-Rojo's *The Repeating Island*, the time in 1962 when the world seemed about to explode in a nuclear catastrophy over Cuba as a result of a confrontation between the U.S and the USSR. The author effectively juxtaposes excerpts of the dramatic speeches made by John F. Kennedy (139) and Fidel Castro ("Los ex-ter-mi-na-ros," 143). Seldom has a scene been so powerfully rendered, one where the reader senses, as the novel comes to an open end, that it is a profound meditation on a small ("underdeveloped") country caught in a tug-of-war between two world powers. The Castro that emerges in his own words matches the one Greene observed (see *Collected Essays* 304). Castro is playing a role on the world stage. He, too, like the narrator, is a Quixotic clown figure whose only strength is the power of his words, his words alone ("Ready for anything. He's mad," 143).

Closure is brought with the disappearance of the threat of annihilation, as if by miracle. Benítez-Rojo had implied the word "miracle," as well, meaning something enduring in the Cuban spirit that makes the Apocalypse something foreign to the Cuban way of life. Desnoes concurs, but qualifies the word Apocalypse with an alternative word, Utopia. That is the belief that deep down sustains the narrator, starting with his choice to stay behind while his family and friends left.

Beyond its initial representation of a barren land that replicates a commonplace setting of modernity by the literary sources that inspired him, Desnoes extends the reflection on the demise of myth in the modern age begun by T.S.Eliot's *The Waste Land*. He addresses the relationship beetwern the American Dream and his native land and finds in Hemingway's house the symbol of colonial entrapment that validated the Revolution; and he also finds a blindside to the Revolution when it canonizes a myth that meant its dispossession.

Desnoes dismisses Hemingway as the personification of a narcissistic myth which leaves potential destruction in its wake when the individual mistakenly looks at himself or herself in its mirror (the pool scene and Elena). But Desnoes's style and use of the iceberg theory and the objective correlative are learned from Hemingway, the writer. Their agency for clearsightedness epitomized in the extended visit to Hemingway's house underscores the narrator's faulty, unreliable vision of him at the time he called him "a second-rate artist" (82).

He pays homage to Graham Greene. Besides the connections earlier suggested, in the end Desnoes paints an Everyman ("I'm a mediocre man, a modern man, a link in the chain, a worthless cockroach," 152) whose desultory life is redeemed by his very meekness and apparent irrelevancy in the revolutionary society. In the *La Jiribilla* interview, Desnoes says:

> Para mí, de *Memorias del subdesarollo* lo más importante es la ambigüedad. El asunto no es estar a favor o en contra, sino hacer pensar, reflexionar, no tener una sola posición. Creo que esa es la razón por la cual los jóvenes se identifican con la obra, le dio un espacio a otras visiones menos cerradas, dogmáticas, fanáticas.

(To me, what's most important in *Inconsolable Memories* is its ambiguity. Its subject is not to be for or against, but to provoke thinking, reflection, and not hold to one single position. I think that's the reason why the young identify with the book; it provides space for other, less closed, dogmatic and fanatical visions.)

Like Wormold, the *gusano* narrator is associated with an organic element needed for reproduction (*guano*, excrement used as fertilizer). More than Greene, in fact, whose vocabulary is qualified by religious overtones (however profane), when transcendence is achieved by the likes of Querry, the whisky priest, and others, Desnoes's stress on his narrator's symbolic approximation to manure is effective in associating him with a regenerative element of the soil.

Desnoes subtly suggests an ending belied by the surface appearance of a society and an individual still adrift; but one that is very close to all the writers discussed in this book: their sense of the Caribbean grounded in cyclical elements that outlast History.

Chapter Nine
Seeing the Light: *Elena and her Friend*

Just as the photograph of El Lider in *Dreaming in Cuban*, and the missing wife's in *The Old Man the Sea*, are symbolic of an absent individual that objectifies a gazer's sense of loss which is self-consciously borne and transcended in action, there are two pictures in light and shadow at the center of this book that, with the passing of time, stand for loss that is yet overcome because their subjects are being given permanence in this book. To be sure, Celia's loss is Gustavo; and Santiago's is his youth told in works of fiction. The loss and affirmation addressed in this closing chapter are fixed in the photographs of two individuals, Elena and her friend, and what they personify.

Both Garcia and Hemingway put to effective use the aesthetic principle of the objective correlative: an image was chosen to represent, and neutralize, an emotion. I, too, see an emotion in the two photos taken of Elena and her friend on the terrace of a restaurant on *La Rampa* in Central Havana on the afternoon of Monday February 10, 2003. Elena's friend remains nameless, her faint smile matches her self-effacing presence which inversely serves the purpose of emphasizing Elena's broad smile and forwarding presence. I can see now how both are at the center of my memory of their country.

I recall noticing Elena waitressing at a table not far from ours, and her friend standing nearby. Taking a break after bringing the bill and chatting with the diners, she joined her friend in a shaded spot on a corner of the terrace. They were chatting while glancing at the street. I got up and asked them if they minded having their picture taken. Both smiled their consent. Then, as I rejoined my wife at our table, Elena came out of the shade, with her friend following her, into the bright light of the terrace with a look of intense curiosity and a lingering smile. I picked up my camera and said I would take a second picture in the brighter light. I got it and we began to chat. I said that my wife and I were from Canada, and that our stay in Cuba was about to come to an end. I asked them whether they wanted copies of the pictures. Elena's friend indifferently shook her head. Elena, smiling broadly, said yes. I looked for a piece of paper and a pen. She wrote down her name, "Ellen Thomson." She went on to write her address but she was uncertain about the postal code. Seeing the English connotation of her name, I said to her she must be of Jamaican or Barbadian parentage. She said no. I insisted: "But with a name like Thomson you must be of West Indian English parentage." She again said she did not know.

I noticed when she wrote down "Ellen" she said it in Spanish, "Elena." I liked the sound and chose to remember her by that name.

She asked us when we would come back to Cuba. I said soon, my wife said maybe in a year. I don't recall that we went on with the conversation since the bill had come. We paid (not without noticing that our older, maternal-looking waitress had taken $4 off the top, her self-serving tip) and got up. I heard Elena compliment my wife for her dress. The last that I saw of her was her wide, warm smile when we said goodbye and added "Vaya con dios" for our safe return to our country and hers. She replied, in turn, "Vaya con dios!"

A week after we returned to Canada I sent her a short note along with copies of the pictures for her to share with her friend; and to let us know the moment she received them. That was on February 21. We never heard from Elena. Mail is reportedly slow in Cuba. We were told that two months is not an unusual time for a letter to get to Canada from Cuba. It has been considerably more than two months now, closer to a year. Maybe the letter never reached her, which is not uncommon. Maybe if we return to Havana, we'll look her up at the restaurant on *La Rampa*, if she is still working there. Or we'll try to reach her at her East Havana address, if she is still in Cuba. The likelihood of failing to find her because she was no longer in Cuba might be more certain.

She probably secured her way out of the island, like so many of her peers, by marrying a foreigner, hopefully out of love, but surely in hope of a better future abroad.

* * *

I know nothing of Elena, neither her age, background, nor anything else. What I know is what I see reflected in her pictured gaze. And I am grateful. Hers isn't the other Helen's gaze that reduced Derek Walcott's narrator to speechlessness in his epic narrative of a return journey to the land of his birth: "...that incredible/ stare paralyzed me past any figure of speech" (*Omeros* 1.6.3). I am not sure, however, that just as Walcott's narrator resorted to similes (Helen of Troy) and metaphors (she is a "panther," *Ibid*. ff.) to try to name the vision that struck him, I am left with a better alternative. There is a strong chance that I am: she is *pictured*. (Walcott's Helen is never physically described, hence *seen*; because the narrator is blinded by the sun radiating from her.) In Merleau-Ponty's language, she is a "body image" (206), thus the location of perception, mine. What do I see? And what does what I see tell me about myself (to paraphrase Merleau-Ponty: "I perceive therefore I am")?

In the first picture, Elena is frankly looking at the camera from a shaded spot. Her smile, wide eyes and self-assurance are on a par with her slightly tilted head, joined hands and her leaning posture on a pillar. Her friend is in the background, her head turned to apparently see what is being called to her attention. Her body turned sideways marginalizes her presence.

Light in that photo is shaded, and it suggests repose, casualness and hospitality. The two stone pillars are like a doorway at the center of which stands Elena in a welcoming posture. As the second photo reveals in brighter light, this supposed doorway is not an entrance but a portal to the world outside the restaurant. The two waitresses in both photos are hostesses resting after their nurturing activities.They fed their guests and are confident of their success standing inside the portal. They restored their guests to face the world outside with its hustle and bustle (the passing car, the passers-by).

In the opening photo, Elena's dominant presence is acknowledged by her friend's side glance of curiosity. Her friend is standing near a palm tree which overshadows her. Elena is at a remove from the center of the shadow, at a distance that suggests self-reliance, independence from the sheltering palm tree. Her leaning on the stone pillar sets her apart from the natural world and identifies her sense of comfort with urban architecture. In fact, she is framed by the palm tree in the background and the potted plant on the right side of the pillar. She is encircled by two symbols of organicity. Her presence is one controlled or harmonized by the natural world that accounts in part for her confidently leaning on the stone pillar.

In fact, the second photo adds another frame: that of the two stone pillars. Elena emerges from the natural frame of plants of the first photo and, in the second one, moves into the man-made frame of the stone pillars. She has not lost her poise in either photo; she appears at ease in both. The dual frame brings out the focus on her self-confident gaze, her whole body is in a relaxed position highlighted by her smile which merely confirms what her body language says: "I know who I am. I am at ease in the natural and in the man-made world. I am the catalyst of opposites. I unite the contraries. I am young and strong. I can take care of myself."

She is dressed in the uniform of her trade which appears to be unnatural: the jacket is ill-fitting, it opens on her waist, and her bow tie is askew. Her arms and face dismiss her accouterment as an imposed, ordered requirement akin to the uniform of schoolchildren. It is no match for what it fails to cover up: the exuberance of her smile, the confidence of her wide eyes and the freedom of her bare arms. The casual confidence of her posture leaning against the stone pillar identifies how she effortlessly stands apart from the restrictions of a dress code and those of the social realm symbolized by the pillars. But there is more.

Elena's name mythologically represents *light* (it is the sun for Walcott adapting the Homeric glitter of "the face that launched a thousand ships"). Her smile is a light that shimmers in a shaded setting. The colors of her accouterment or dress code are generally dark: the bow tie, the skirt, the jacket. They altogether overshadow the glaring whiteness of her blouse. The mix of light and dark in dress apparently conveys a disharmony, a contradiction, when placed in juxtaposition with the dark and light-skinned color of the two friends' physical appearance.

They are at ease with each other. None is at ease in the uniform of their trade. As waitresses, they are socially-dressed commodities. Beyond their imposed identities, both their smiles and relative self-confidence suggest that they are more than meets the eye gazing at their uniform.

The shaded setting and contrasting distance between the two friends in the first photo are noticeably changed in the second. They are closer not simply to the camera but to each other; in fact they are at an equal distance, shoulder to shoulder, in a setting dominated by light in the foreground and background. They are equally centered as individual selves different in skin color --which seems to be immaterial to friendship, but material for what each inner self reveals in body language. Elena's smile softly shimmers in the first photo; in the second, it is brightly shining. Her standing straight matches the firmness of her gaze, her arms are loose alongside her body, her eyes are focused and direct. Everything about her says boldness, self-assurance, strength. Her friend's smile has brightened. She, too, has come forward but her eyes remain somewhat shy and diffident; still, they convey a gentle look. She appears as a "kid sister" to Elena (who is taller). Her smile does not match Elena's: it is faint compared to Elena's radiancy. Her posture is reclusive and she generally projects an air of wistfulness. Either way, the opposite is true for Elena.

The pictured gaze of Elena and her friend suggests a rapport between individual selves; one where balance is struck by complementarity in height, physical appearance, age (Elena appears to be older than her friend) and complexion. Just as the emergence of natural light provides a sharper representation of the pictured gaze in the second photo, other elements in the natural setting appear.

The organic world of trees and leaves, obscured in the first photo, is noticeably present in the brightly lit garden beneath the terrace and across the street. Though nature is in the background and no longer a frame, its brightness correlates with the forwardness of Elena's body language. It is bold, alert, readily assertive and symbolized by the directness of her gaze and assertiveness of her smile. Standing straight, her shoulders are squared for self-reliance and the outer light of her smile glitters. The inner light of her character is objectified by the sunlit patches behind her, namely the one that splashes on the leaning tree directly behind her. The combination of the light and the leaning tree in the second photo naturally correlates with a notable feature in the first one, Elena leaning on a pillar. She already was the light shining in the shadow.

The second photo naturally interconnects with the previous one in a number of additional ways. Out of the shadow of the first photo emerge the two friends standing next to each other as embodiments of light. Their light is more than the natural sunlit patches; it is the light of friendship uniting them, the naturalness of their being together, balancing complementary complexions, heights, smiles and postures. Both are looking at the camera and show their empathy with the gazer: a forwarding one for Elena and a self-effacing one for her friend. Their gaze sends out a welcoming message.

Admittedly, Elena's figuration stands out compared to her friend's. She is indeed the older, experienced sister who has taken her "kid sister" under her wing. She leads her from the obscured background to the brightness of full light. Yet, though Elena's association with light connects her to her mythic namesake, there is no hint in her look of what left Walcott's narrator dumbfounded and speechless. Hers is not a blinding, intimidating --and even threatening-- light. Quite the opposite.

But I am grateful that Walcott articulated the central issue of "home" for the wandering Caribbean man by problematizing the metaphor of light and the difficult terms of its absorption by a colonized self. Because I know that for Walcott the light is both Helen and St.Lucia, his birthplace, I am able to perceive in Elena the archetypal image of not just one island's light but that of the Caribbean as a whole. Elena could be a Haitian "Hélène." However, I did not travel to Haiti but to Cuba, and my felt experience of the country --with all five senses alive-- was one of feeling at home. Cuba was another home for the Caribbean light indifferently named Helen, Ellen, Hélène or Elena. Elena's gaze was beyond metaphor ("When would I enter that light beyond metaphor?" *Omeros* 6.54.3). It meant, "That's me." Period. A gaze that reduced questions to nothingness: "What does it matter that I am of West Indian British heritage or not? What does it matter if my name is Ellen Thomson? And that I am Cuban? Can't you see me?"

And so I was taught that afternoon on *La Rampa* that I could see. And I learned that Elena was our Caribbean light.

I discovered that Elena represented everything that attaches one to the country of his/her birth, and that it is a shared experience irrespective of generation, gender and nationality. In her, I saw what Walcott meant when his narrator is restored to true speech: "See her there, my mother, my grandmother, my great-great-/grandmother. See the black ants of their sons,/ their coal-carrying mothers. Feel the shame, the self-hate/ draining from all our bodies" (*Omeros* 6.48.3).

Elena will last because of what her pictured gaze stands for. This is our gain in the Caribbean, and we are grateful. What more can one ask of a gaze through which one learned so much? Like so many in our time, fragmented and looking for a home of our own, I saw the Caribbean light. Cubans were convinced I was one of theirs, and a customs officer was beyond the need for convincing. Her smile set all interrogations aside.

I see her and her friend's pictured gaze basking in a vision of light.

Conclusion

Can there be an ending to this book? A farewell perhaps, and certainly a lingering belief in the ongoing life of a people fixed in photos of its unique diversity, sense of self and resiliency. Hopefully, the opening photos of the young on José Martí Day captured the dilemma of an island struggling with the shadow of History interwoven with natural sunlight.

How can the man-made construct of History continue melding with natural elements in daily living, adapting the cycle of life to a carousel, when faced with the very real impediments of food rationing and restrictions on individual rights? How is immutability in ideology to survive the mutability of the aging fathers of the Revolution, not simply in temporal terms, but already in the direction taken toward development and increased foreign investment, identified as a "pact with the devil" (Fidel Castro quoted in *Afro-Cuban Voices* viii)?

These are vexing questions, yet the responses to them are not readily apparent. The writings analyzed in this book suggest that Cuba has been visited in its history by worse threats than tourism, and prevailed. Its capacity to survive stems from a vision that is other than the merely political. The Cuban missile crisis of 1962, for example, is Benítez-Rojo's and Desnoes's example of the culture's organic resistance even to the specter of the Apocalypse. The use of the body metaphor by Garcia, Hemingway, Iyer and Desnoes highlights the reality of a land victimized by patriarchy that is, nonetheless, redeemed by individuals whose lives deconstruct a form of heroism tied to the male body. Garcia's Reina, Hemingway's Santiago, Iyer's Lourdes, Greene's Wormold and Desnoes's anti-hero redefine their bodies as an act of choice. The steady gaze of Celia, Pilar, Reina, Santiago, Lourdes, Desnoes's narrator and Elena emblematizes the silent but eloquent resiliency of the individual caught in pictures and literature belying the misuse of language.

However, the re-emergence of hustlers and hookers (*jineteros* and *jineteras*) in contemporary Havana is a daunting, but not unexpected, throwback to the pre-revolutionary years. The "sexual exchange" or "chief commerce of the city" noted by a character in Greene's 1958 novel, *Our Man in Havana* (56), seems to have withstood the passing of time in hotels like the Habana Libre, the Nacional, in Central Havana, or the Inglaterra, in Old Havana, as well as on the streets and in various restaurants throughout the city, and even shopping at Miramar's *supermercados* (high-priced, dollar supermarkets). The sex traffic on Malecón drive moves on day and night. A commercial staple before the Revolution, it is a fact of daily living now that the Revolution has turned to tourism once more for badly-needed revenue.

* * *

My point in drawing attention to the quotidianness and omnipresence of prostitution is the critical depth it adds to a previous chapter's focus on "the gazed body." The sex traffic is part of a familiar urban landscape that backdrops Georgina Herrera and Alden Knight's comments, discussed later.

The representation of the body as a commodity is contextualized by Garcia in *The Agüero Sisters* in Dulce's marginalization from her family and society, thereby leaving her the single option of selling her body to escape their restrictions. But as she finds her way to Spain, and later rejoins her mother in Miami, her body seems to be out of control: "It was hell to get here. I needed seven hundred dollars for the flight, and so for three endless days, I resorted to my old Havana tricks. I try to tell myself it doesn't matter, that it's always a means, not an end. But when the hell will I ever stop needing the means" (285)?

For Garcia, prostitution is the most sinister early results of the "pact with the devil." Yet, the last thoughts entertained by Dulce, who finds work in a sandwich shop in Miami, are a reflection on the broader meaning of prostitution in a market economy. As it satisfies material needs in "hard times," it keeps the closeness of nothingness at a distance: "I ate a sandwich like that once in Cuba, years ago, before the hard times hit. It made me realize how close we are to forgetting everything, how close we are to not existing at all" (288). That last point is corroborated by Herrera and Knight in *Afro-Cuban Voices*.

Though Georgina Herrera, a writer, and Alden Knight, an actor, are speaking in the same time period as the publication of Garcia's novel, they do not reflect on the "loss of control" reversing the sense of control they see in prostitution (and that Dulce affirms early in the novel: "*Sex is the only thing* they can't ration in Havana. It's the next-best currency after dollars, and much more democratic, if you ask me," 51). For Herrera, prostitution is a young woman's choice for empowerment in a marketplace dominated by the search for U.S. dollars: "That's why...for a young, intelligent woman to go out and give her body to bring food home for her family and for herself, she has to have very high self-esteem, she has to be very sure of what her values are and what she's going after" (124). Alden Knight, on the other hand, links prostitution and a resurgent racism attendant to mass tourism. Confirming the findings of De la Fuente (*A Nation for All*, 318-322), he, too, sees disenfranchisement meted out to Afro-Cubans and mulattos in the service sector catering to primarily white tourists. For him, prostitution is less a matter left to individual choice than a *sine qua non* outlet for survival. Present conditions being as they are, Knight does not see what Garcia suggests in the aftermath of "survival," when the prostitute's body is out of control:

In the international press what is most commented on is that the prostitutes are only black and mulatto women, and when I see young black women with middle-aged or older men, I reflect and say to myself, "OK, take her, so you know what it's like!" What I mean to say is that I don't criticize the women....

Black and mulatto women have more trouble finding work, whether from a Cuban or a foreigner, because, although they're qualified, they're not seen to be the ideal choice. They're not the right Western type. (114)

In addition, neither Herrera nor Knight addresses a common worldwide fallout from the sex trade: the spread of AIDS. (It is hinted at by Garcia. It may be because Dulce knows she is sereopositive that she rejects her mother's wish that she have a child, and mutters: "I don't tell her either, that I've been bleeding in between periods for months," 286).

* * *

Throughout the month I spent in Cuba, reading the official line in newspapers, watching public affairs programs on the state-run television, listening to reports on the many international conferences that took place in Havana, there was not a single public reference to AIDS that I can recall (nor to prostitution for that matter; though there was an anti-drug campaign). In conversations, my interlocutors' response to the fact of prostitution was unanimously tolerant and echoed Herrera's and Knight's points of view.

To me, the silence over AIDS parallels the one over the implications of the "pact with the devil" underlying the idea of progress and development tied to mass tourism. What the State's notion of progress hides emerges in the self-destructiveness of prostitution that is also kept hidden. Yet, there is a doubling in the metaphor of the body of the individual and of the State from Cristina Garcia's and Pico Iyer's viewpoints. *The Agüero Sisters* and *Cuba and the Night* stand out as contemporary texts focused on Cuba that draw attention to the interrelatedness of social and individual trends crippling the option taken on the Faustian myth, and upon which hangs so much of Cuba's future.

Prostitution, alleged renascent racism, mass tourism, totalitarian rule, an aging political leadership, rampant obsession with the U.S. dollar in all walks of life, and rumblings of dissidence are some of the sore points of present-day Cuba, and they cast a shadow over the future faced by the young in the words and pictures of this book. As a matter of fact, the problems summed up above are for more than one writer not "sore points" but doom-like signs spelling out an apocalyptic ending:

"I am often asked what Castro's future will be," famed, exile Cuban author Guillermo Cabrera Infante wrote in 1992. "I always answer that he has none: He spent it all on his urge to keep himself in power." It is clear that Castro will do little that risks sacrificing control....Meanwhile, defying decades of predictions, Castro lurches on, a man who, in the words of his 40th-anniversary speech, "dresses the same, who thinks the same, who dreams the same" as the day he came down from the Sierra Maestra. (Elizabeth Newhouse, *Cuba* 212)

Yet, I am reminded of Roger Dorsinville's praise of Fidel Castro for granting citizenship to 500,000 impoverished Haitians in the early days of the Revolution, and of my meeting Sixto, one of their descendants, and of my gratitude for the guidance he provided in Havana. He, his wife Maria and their children, and other ordinary Cubans like Gracia and Elena, will always be remembered for greeting me like family. Without them I would not have understood Benítez-Rojo's gazing at the two women one seemingly apocalyptic day during the 1962 missile crisis (*Ibid.* 10). A positive closure to *Understanding Contemporary Cuba in Visual and Verbal Forms* can only be open-ended like the society's future seen as resting not on one man, albeit an icon of the Revolution, but on the timeless resiliency of the people's *carnaval* Benítez-Rojo celebrates:

Think of the dancing flourishes, the rhythms of the conga, the samba, the masks, the hoods, the men dressed and painted as women, the bottles of rum, the sweets, the confetti and colored streamers, the hubbub, the carousal, the flutes, the drums, the cornet and the trombone, the teasing, the jealousy, the whistles and the faces, the razor that draws blood, death, life, reality in forward and reverse, torrents of people who flood the streets, the night lit up like an endless dream, the figure of a centipede that comes together and then breaks up, that winds and stretches beneath the ritual's rhythm, that flees the rhythm without escaping it, putting off its defeat, stealing off and hiding itself, imbedding itself finally in the rhythm, always in the rhythm, the beat of the chaos of the islands. (*Ibid.* 29)

And reflecting on the predominance of the motif of the look in writings on Cuba from Garcia to Desnoes linked to the mainstream of modernity in phenomenology, photography and literature, I am left with their lasting commitment to the articulation of vision and truth tied to a redefinition of language rooted in the culture itself. The resulting image of Cuba is, then, akin to the renewed faith in art and language that inspired the rise of Modernism against the backdrop of historical calamities that have characterized our times.

The age of Empire and two World Wars backgrounded the writings of Joseph Conrad, Jean-Paul Sartre, Maurice Merleau-Ponty and T.S. Eliot, and the photographs of Henri-Cartier Bresson. These facts of history and their connection with the rise of Modernism are part of a universal memory shared by Cristina

Garcia, Derek Walcott, Graham Greene, Pico Iyer, Edmundo Desnoes and, of course, Ernest Hemingway. The task these writers committed themselves to as artists is the honest representation of Cuba as a familiar worldwide terrain, "a heap of broken images" that each writer worked at restoring. One cannot but find hope in their inscription of Cuba in the mainstream of modernity when Derek Walcott's words are recalled:

> Break a vase and the love that reassembles the fragments is stronger than that love which took its symmetry for granted when it was whole....Antillean art is this restoration of our shattered histories, our shards of vocabulary, our archipelago becoming a synonym for pieces broken off from the original continent. (*The Antilles* n.p.)

Appendices

A. **Nationalism and Consumerism**

The relationship between Canada and Cuba can be defined as one of sympathy and friendship best exemplified by the late Canadian Prime Minister Pierre Elliott Trudeau who visited Cuba on several occasions and whose funeral in Montreal, in 2000, was attended by Fidel Castro. Confirmation of the ties between the two countries can be seen on a plaque in the terminal of the new José Martí International Airport inaugurated in 1997 by then Prime Minister Jean Chrétien. The airport, whose construction was financed by the Canadian International Development Agency, is perhaps the most visible sign of Canada's economic assistance to Cuba, next to various aid projects and exchange programs. But the truly most visible sign of Canada's presence in Cuba occurs on a seasonal level; when large numbers of Canadians, fleeing their country's winter cold, flock to the island's resorts, lured by inexpensive package tours.

Yet, it is in connection with Canada's largest French-speaking province, Quebec, with its recurrent nationalist unrest, that the Canada-Cuba linkage takes its most dramatic form. One phase of nationalist eruption in Quebec in 1970 led to the granting of asylum in Cuba to a number of dissidents, an arrangement brokered by the Canadian government. Socio-cultural developments tied to nationalism and a rising consumerism in Quebec during the nineteen sixties were behind the dissidents' flight to Cuba. These developments are surveyed in this closing essay that looks at events involving Quebec and the Third World dating back to more than a quarter of a century.

My aim in reprinting an old, albeit revised, essay is to direct attention to another way of understanding contemporary Cuba's gamble with what Fidel Castro has termed a "pact with the devil": the adoption of market economy strategies by his socialist and nationalist regime. To look at modern Quebec coming at the crossroads of a choice between nationalism and consumerism in the nineteen sixties, in my opinion, is to see in an enlarged rearview mirror contemporary Cuba's quandary when faced with the same apparent opposite ideologies.

Admittely, an attempted linkage between Cuba --a rigidly controlled sovereign socialist State-- and Quebec --a province of the sovereign Canadian federation-- takes some nerve (my demotic way of anticipating resistance to the very idea of lumping societies that are seemingly worlds apart [conceptually that is] in a common discourse-- though, as shown by Jean-Daniel Lafond, in his documentary film, *L'Heure de Cuba*, no resistance is apparent when the subject is tourism and formal and informal bonding links the average Quebec vacationer and the Cuban service employee since the nineteen eighties, if not earlier).

To be sure, the essay that I am reprinting below might have remained in the particular niche of Quebec history it initially addressed, were it not for my being compelled to reflect on Cuba's turn to mass tourism and its implications for change. What I saw in Cuba in 2003 was like reliving what I detected since the 1960 election of the Liberal Party to power in Quebec, and that of the *Parti Québécois* subsequently in 1976: a confrontation between the apparent opposites of nationalism and consumerism in the course of a society's aspirations.

The central issue relating Quebec and Cuba is what I take to be the very real dilemma represented by the maintenance of the concept of group solidarity (nationalism) against the growing call for better living conditions and civil rights (consumerism) in Cuba. These contraries do not necessarily cancel each other out, but they result in change or co-optation of one by the other as seen in Quebec society since 1960. Consumerism covered up by nationalism (or vice versa) is the trump card played in various provincial elections by the sovereignist *Parti Québécois* from inception in 1967 (see its founder's credo, René Lévesque's *Option Québec*), earning it the electorate's majority support in 1976 reduced to a minority twice since; most recently in April 2003. The Liberal party, which since 1980 has alternately replaced the *Parti Québécois* in the governance of Quebec, appears to be a more successful manifestation of what I call "ideological co-optation"; i.e. the political capacity of responding to a society's call for modernity by putting in place strategies of balance between polarities.

Both Quebec's and Cuba's history are inescapably related in asymmetry of a problematical sort due to each society's minority status in an English-speaking majority northern hemisphere wedded to the capitalist system. As a consequence, I see, at best, the lesson of the Quebec experience to be akin to a road map for Cuba's future direction. At worst, resistance to change becomes counter-productive and makes for an apocalyptic ending that Benítez-Rojo addressed and rejected in 1962.

* * *

The motif of the look that runs throughout this book cannot but benefit from the wider perspective supplied by the Quebec example. No ordinary Cuban is blind to the sight of tourists gazing at them, of whom Cristina Garcia singles out Canadians ("At the next table, a table of sunburnt French Canadians were enjoying baked lobsters and getting drunk on Cuba libres," *Dreaming in Cuban* 223), while Pico Iyer casually lists them among the throngs of foreign visitors to Cuba (*Cuba and the Night* 76, 159-161). Like other foreigners, they represent the consumer market Cubans have been drawn to join. To be sure, the lure of consumerism in Cuba is like a striptease. The tourist gazed at is the stripteaser whose striptease is the tipping that waiters, waitresses and others are ordered to shun but still welcome, while *jineteros* and *jineteras* maneuver in the city for more than tipping. The well-being and sense of comfort the tourists exude are looked at by Cubans in the service sector from an enforced distance. Prostitution, on the other hand, does not recognize boundaries in resort hotels or in the city.

Still, a frustrating distance between the gazer and the gazed exponentially grows in relation with the rise of mass tourism. Discontent sets in and results in the kind of disruption witnessed in the span of one month (March) in 2003, when no less than two planes and one ferryboat were hijacked by individuals seeking to escape to the U.S. in search of better living conditions. To which, the Cuban State's reaction was the arrest and conviction of 75 dissidents, and the summary execution of three of the ferryboat's hijackers.

A hitherto unsuspected -- ironic were it not, in fact, tragic-- additional link between Cuba and Canada is now provided by the example of individuals whom the Cuban State labeled "terrorists," like the individuals the Canadian government similarly labeled in 1970 when it brought in the War Measures Act whose immediate effect was the suspension of civil rights in the whole of Canada. Quebec terrorists did have to bear responsibility for the killing of a provincial government minister and the kidnapping of a British Consul, yet they were not summarily shot, and some of them were allowed to seek asylum in Cuba. In April 2003, the Cuban State ordered the death of three hijackers who had not killed anyone.

As the following essay suggests, the central issue is not the accuracy of terming someone a "dissident" or a "terrorist" in either Canada or Cuba. It is the confrontation of ideological polarities in the construction of modernity in societies not necessarily defined as nation-states, but which define themselves within the framework of a nation-state. I argue, therefore, that the tug-of-war between nationalism and consumerism, from a metaphorical and dialectical perspective, plays itself out in the balance sought between group and individual rights in Quebec as in Cuba.

* * *

Quebec on the Eve of the 15 November 1976 Election

In 1959, Maurice LeNoblet Duplessis died. The death of this politician who had dominated Quebec's political life for three decades signaled the end of an era. Duplessis was the sour incarnation of a long-standing tradition, that of the alliance between the Church and the State which led him to brag that he had bishops eating out of his hands. Duplessis was a politician who clung to quasi-mystical beliefs in the virtues of the past and conceded the present of industrialization and technology to the American trusts and corporations that owned the economy of his province. So that when Duplessis died in Quebec's northern wilderness, while visiting the installations of one of those combines whose rights for exploitation of iron ore were obtained for a pittance, his death was the ironical death of a king [in the words of the late journalist André Laurendeau] a "Negro king."

Knowing his record, intellectuals and artists of Quebec who had formulated their dissent throughout Duplessis' rule in the pages of *Le Devoir* and *Cité Libre* did not cry "Hail to the King" but they thought joyfully nonetheless that their fight against obscurantism had been rewarded. Now, it was felt, Quebec would open its windows to the world. (*Caliban Without Prospero* 27)

During the seventeen years that followed the end of the Duplessis era, it was a commonplace in the thinking in and about Quebec that the evolution of Quebec society was best understood as a quest inspired by the need to open a society that had been traditionally kept closed and isolated. A nation which for better or for worse had been forced to live under conservative ideologies had no alternative but to destroy the frontiers historically established for its protection and survival. The evolution of Quebec over the last seventeen years is thus characterized in a notion that is agreed upon by schools of thought as opposed as that of the Federalists (which believes in Quebec's future within Confederation) and the Independentists (which believes that Quebec's future is best understood within the framework of self-determination). It is precisely on the political dimension of this opening to the world that these two schools of thought disagree.

The problematical frame of this opening to the world is etched by an historical phenomenon during the last decade, in the context of the literature of that period. By means of a singular image in the poetry and fiction of the sixties, the Quebec writer demonstrated a keen interest, if not a fascination, for a diversified and complex cultural experience symbolized by the concept of Negritude. Negritude is an ideology, a literary movement --some would say a mythology-- that grew in the thirties and forties first in Europe and later in Africa and the West Indies. It is a concept argued by intellectuals of the Third World to assert their identity and, by extrapolation, the identity of their native culture. Negritude identified the forms, the characteristics of the cultural experience of black people subjected to colonialism in Africa, the West Indies, as well as the Americas. It is with this search for identity, this quest for self-understanding by Third World intellectuals, that some writers and intellectuals of Quebec associated their vision of a new Quebec. But before analyzing the terms of this new vision we have to consider the ideological conflict which gives it sustenance.

Duplessis' death was accompanied by a crisis within the intelligentsia in Quebec. The intellectual elite revolving around the review *Cité Libre* (1950-1965) led a fight based on a liberal conception of the State and on humanism as an individual code of ethics. Claiming the right to personal fulfillment freed of conservative, religious and other dogmatic impositions, Pierre Elliott Trudeau, Gérard Pelletier and other thinkers perceived the disappearance of the Duplessis era as the symbolic sign of the birth of a society which by discarding a state-of-siege mentality would henceforth relate to the mainstream of modernity:

Around 1960 it seemed that freedom was going to triumph in the end. From 1945 on, a series of events and movements had combined to relegate the traditional concepts of authority in Quebec to the scrap-heap.... So much so that the generation entering its twenties in 1960 was the first in our history to receive fairly complete freedom as its lot. The dogmatism of Church and State, of tradition, of the nation, had been defeated. (Pierre Elliott Trudeau, *Federalism and the French Canadians* 206)

But that elite, nourished by the ideas of the English liberal tradition, the thinking of the French Christian humanists and the social doctrine of the Catholic Church, found itself overtaken by a series of events. On the outside, it was the accession of former colonies in Africa and the West Indies to self-determination. On the inside, this elite was outflanked by upheavals in the political, labor, religious and educational fields. The past was opposed to the present, conservatism to radicalism, resignation to defiance, tradition to innovation. Two world outlooks, two conceptions of the new *Québécois*, were brought to light. So much so that Pierre Elliott Trudeau bemusedly notes that, "In 1960, everything was becoming possible in Quebec, even revolution" (*Ibid.*).

The precepts of liberalism and humanism advocated by the *Cité Libre* elite gave rise to a new social conscience determined to effect a total overhaul of Quebec society. The generation following *Cité Libre*, organized around *Liberté* (1958 -), *Parti Pris* (1963-1968), *Socialisme 64* (1964-1966), and a publishing house like Hexagone, felt free to draw parallels and establish ideological links between the decolonization movement in Africa and Asia and the "Quiet Revolution" that was occurring in Quebec. Instead of the European liberal and humanist model, the intellectuals of *Parti Pris* substituted a Third World model inscribed in the perspective of colonialism, declaring the right of people to control their political destiny. The theorists of *Parti Pris*, far from perceiving Duplessis' rule as an aberration, or as the cause of Quebec's problems, characterized it as the reflection of a historical imbalance consequent to the 1760 Conquest. Accordingly, it was felt that a feeling of dispossession deeply embedded in consciences explained the century-long influence of the Church and the traditional reliance on one form of dogmatism or another in social and individual relations. Taking a long view of the history of Quebec since 1760, these theorists assigned to dispossession the significance of a dramatic shock which traditionally had never been confronted. The young intellectuals of *Parti Pris* committed themselves to the task of bringing about its resolution.

Basically, *Parti Pris*' ideological model meant that, like the former colonies of the Third World, Quebec had to liberate, repossess and recreate itself by means of political sovereignty. The equation was as follows: like the Third World colonies, Quebec had been subjected to a foreign power (England and, by extension, English Canada). A local administration had been put in place (English Canada), controlled by means of indirect rule. Any attempt at questioning the status quo was canceled out from the beginning insofar as a conservative ideology obsessed with the past and a denial of the present dominated in all spheres of activity, and directly or indirectly sustained a colonial type of subjugation. Individual success was achieved by means of assimilation, acculturation to the dominant power group. On the one hand, the masses were kept resigned and ignorant of the real causes of their sense of defeat; on the other hand, an elite was convinced of the need to maintain the status quo as a guarantee of social mobility.

Many other parallels were drawn with the aim of re-enforcing this new vision of Quebec sharing the Third World experience of colonialism, disenfranchisement and alienation. Not surprisingly, we find underlying the thinking of Paul Chamberland, Pierre Vallières, Pierre Maheu and others, some of the key ideas of the revolutionary Martiniquan Frantz Fanon. It is these same ideas, especially Fanon's theories on colonial violence, which in practice inspired the action of the first cells of the FLQ (Quebec Liberation Front) in the early sixties. Read and analyzed further by Pierre Elliott Trudeau, Gérard Pelletier and other intellectuals of both *Cité Libre* and *Parti Pris*, the works of Fanon, and later, Albert Memmi, Jacques Berque, Antonio Gramsci and Ché Guevara, were perceived as the cornerstone of a debate on the future form of Quebec society. Thus, it is with this crisis between two generations in the intelligentsia in the background that we can approach the image centrally used in the literature of Quebec of the sixties, the image of Negritude as co-opted by Quebec writers.

* * *

Admittedly, the identification in Quebec with a Third World experience did not take place on the popular level; it was the concern of an educated middle-class. In its extreme form, that movement erupted in the violence or the rhetoric of violence of the FLQ members or sympathizers during the period 1963-1970. Inasmuch as this violence was not supported by the general population that the terrorists claimed to represent, their action was that of marginal elements in Quebec society. One could even add that insofar as identification with the Third World was essentially a theoretical problem debated by intellectuals in little magazines that reached a restricted readership, the Fanonian model is perhaps doubtful as an empirical base for the analysis of the cultural effervescence of Quebec during the sixties. But, on the literary level, in the mythical perspective of the imagination in Quebec, the shock value of linking with the Third World articulated a dramatic image of the new *Québécois*.

The aesthetics of the *Parti Pris* movement celebrated a native land; it called for an exploration, an inventory of landscape which had to be given proper expression. It established the particularities of a concept of art which rested on the power of the word, the spoken effectiveness of language in its more vital, concrete and direct form. It was a concept of art that aimed at describing in realistic fashion the *Québécois*' everyday life of alienation and general uneasiness. To be sure, that vision produced an art that was violent in language and imagery, since it was coupled with a design that was vital and existential according to its practitioners: the struggle for liberation. In such a context, then, the mythology of Negritude and the image of the black man as the symbol of the *Québécois* were put to use: "I am the evil that you have created. I am what you have created Dorchester, Colburn, Durham. I am the heap of blackness in the gallows of America" (*L'Afficheur hurle* 18, my translation). The influence of the poet, politician and playwright from Martinique, Aimé Césaire, was dominant in this literature of "decolonization."

The perception of the black man did not differ from a form of stereotyping that stood for what the onlooker aimed at finding in what was looked at. To that extent, it revealed a psychological truth far more germane to the onlooker than the one that was looked at. And perhaps that is what needs to be underlined: how the *Québécois* "engagé" writer painted a reverse image which he claimed as his own. This process of identification was fairly simple: the *Québécois* was perceived as uprooted, oppressed and divorced from himself --in Sartrean terms, someone who existed for others rather than for himself. He was therefore associated with the image of the black, the stereotyped image of the alienated being. The writers expressing with the greatest anguish their sense of unease went to the extent of co-opting even the blackness of pigmentation to express their alienation, if not the precise historical experiences meted out to the black man: "When I'll go to New York it is to Harlem that I will head for and not because of exoticism. I am much too concerned with precise familial links. I know the feeling of nightsticks in Alabama. There are fraternities in sorrows that your civil rights cannot hide" (*L'Afficheur hurle* 59). If the black man represented in his concrete, physical self the embodiment of dispossession, the Quebec writer of the sixties affirmed that the *Québécois* was a "white nigger" because he displayed all the psychological characteristics of Negritude (Pierre Vallières, *Nègres blancs d'Amérique* 25 ff.*).*

The metaphor of Negritude was omnipresent in the literature of the sixties. In 1962, the novelist Jacques Godbout, fresh from a two-year stay in Ethiopia, used a tropical colonial setting in *L'Aquarium* on the periphery of which a motley crew of expatriates survived. Clearly, that novel was symbolic of Godbout's perception of Quebec as a hothouse environment for which fresh air was needed. Another writer, Réal Benoît, in a long short story entitled *Rhum Soda*, used Haitian culture to evoke a sense of personal freedom sorely lacking in the Quebec experience. But it was particularly in the writings of Hubert Aquin (*Prochain épisode, Trou de mémoire*), Paul Chamberland (*Terre Québec, L'Afficheur hurle*), Jacques Renaud (*Le Cassé*), Jacques Brault, Gaston Miron, Gérald Godin and Michèle Lalonde, to name just the major writers of the period, that we can see how this new-found mythology was put to use. In her poem *Speak White*, published in 1968, Michèle Lalonde addressed an imaginary English audience:

Speak white/ Tell us again about freedom and democracy/ We know that liberty is a black word/ as misery is black/ as blood is muddied with the dust of Algiers or of Little Rock/ Speak white from Westminster to Washington, take turns/ Speak white as on Wall Street/ white as in Watts/ Be civilized/ and understand our conventional answer/ when you ask us politely/ how do you do/ and we mean to reply/ we're doing all right/ we're doing fine/ we/ are not alone/ We know that we are not alone. (*Speak White* 29,31)

What we have in this passage is a summary of the equation drawn by most writers of the sixties, an equation between what is said to have been the historical experience of the Québécois and that of other minority groups throughout the world, especially Blacks.

In more general terms, the new mythology expressed itself as a lyrical and aggressive call for revolution, armed uprising. It drew the picture of the Quebec revolutionary whose archetype was the Fanonian colonized who finds liberation by means of cathartic violence. In the words of Paul Chamberland: "The foundries are erupting in the veins of a people/ the majestic soil grows and carves in its flesh/ the hammer and the/ sickle and the cannon powder/ its face expands in the primordial lights of bombs" (*Terre Québec* 33). Elsewhere, it was the clinical description of a quotidian lifestyle bared of any artifice, where an individual dispossessed of self-identity, language and culture, sought a precise object to vent his rage. That was the substance of Jacques Renaud's *Le Cassé*. Further, it was a psychological climate where the *Québécois* was described as a member of the international fraternity of the "wretched of the earth." That was the design of Hubert Aquin's *Prochain épisode*.

* * *

Basically, there are two salient features to the Negritude archetype: first, an inventory of a sense of uneasiness and pain, the quest through myriad events for the causes of a state of despair; second, following the identification of unease and anguish, a desire to act upon and perhaps correct this state of despair. In Quebec literature of the sixties we find therefore by means of characterization, symbolism and themes, the commitment of the writer to a refusal of traditional acceptance and resignation. His commitment was to revolt and to the depiction of augurs of the birth of a new revolutionary being. A novel that captured those two attitudes is Jacques Godbout's *Le Couteau sur la table* (1965). In the poetry of Paul Chamberland, revolt was dramatized in a symbolism of blood and fire suggestive of a ritual of destruction accompanied by creation. In Chamberland as well as Miron, the theme was the cry of pain preceding the ultimate release in anger.

But around 1968 the movement of revolt and identification with the Third World had spent itself. The magazine *Parti Pris* folded. The principal theorists of the movement had other concerns. Chamberland left for Paris to pursue his studies. Upon his return, and with the collaboration of Pierre Maheu, he became involved in mysticism and in research on language and communications. Chamberland and the former revolutionaries found themselves in sympathy with the counter-culture and other popular movements coming from the U.S. which were proclaiming by the end of the sixties that social change could best be achieved by means of psychic change. Hubert Aquin, who in his first novel-- *Prochain épisode*-- was already engaged in extending the boundaries of experimental fiction, went on to further mystify his readers with a display of arcane erudition and a probing of the mysteries of identity. The rhetoric of disguise, metamorphosis, bewildering temporal and spatial schemes, demonstrated Aquin's affinities with the baroque tradition. Other writers cultivated an interest in the visual arts, in cinema for instance. Or they simply stopped writing.

By the Fall of 1970, as in a final resurgence, the FLQ broke in the news; but it was more or less to signal its death throes. Two years earlier, the visionaries and celebrants of a revolutionary Quebec had revealed they were tired or defeated. Why and how?

Perhaps it was the revenge of history; a revenge not altogether different from the one that the *Parti Pris* generation had taken against their elders of *Cité Libre*. Toward the end of the sixties a new generation was no longer conditioned by the negative impositions at the root of the revolt of *Parti Pris*. In an urban Quebec, where the birth rate reached zero degree, the traditional family no longer existed. The Church had lost its former power; the secondary and college school systems were secularized; a breath of fresh air blowing all over Quebec since 1960 brought in its wake the sequels of the decolonization movement in Africa.

The process of self-determination in most of the former colonies suffered from false starts or it was aborted by ethnic struggles and coups d'état. Also, those newly-independent nations discovered they were stilll very much dependent on the resources of the former colonizing powers. Mainly, the rebellion against the established order in Quebec found a substitute to Fanon in the youth movement, rock music and "flower power": a youth movement or counter-culture which proclaimed the need for change by means of inner quest and experimentation with drugs. The stress was on personal rather than collective vision.

In Quebec, as well as in the United States, England and France, the new generation that appeared in the late sixties replaced the hardline political models for social change with so-called alternative models (albeit provided by the culture of affluence and consumerism). Pop culture characterized the era. The new heroes were the Beatles, the Rolling Stones and other media favorites. The Third World model for revolt was discarded and a revolt more germane to the North American experience was in place, the product of the contradictions of the consumer society. Violence or the rhetoric of violence was no longer fashionable, but "dropping out" of the system was. The talk was no longer about removal *of* the system but removal *from* the system. Hence a whole generation turned to utopias: it was back to nature, getting close to the earth, indulgence in Eastern philosophies, recourse to communal lifestyle.

An anarchic wind blew over the European and North American youth of that period, and Quebec youth --the very same generation which presumably should have continued the fight begun by *Parti Pris*-- participated in the process.

There was a general lack of interest in *society*. Instead of Fanon, the taste was for Jimi Hendrix. Janice Joplin was deemed more significant than Angela Davis. Quebec perhaps had finally made its entry into the modern world when the post-*Parti Pris* counter-culturists, grouped around the avant-garde little magazine *Mainmise* (founded in 1970), identified Quebec's problems with the general malaise prevailing in most industrialized Western societies.

The malaise was the same, and the remedy provided in Quebec, as in the U.S. and elsewhere, was the recourse to, at best, self-articulated, private and peaceful values; and, at worst, hallucinatory solutions. The sentiment of dispossession which for the *Parti Pris* generation had been a root motivation of the need for social change was now identified with an overwhelming sense of despair and cultural decadence prevalent throughout the Western world. There was polarization between the youth and avant-garde intellectuals claiming the counter-culture and the middle-class Establishment. On the other hand, the Quebec Establishment rejoiced in finding itself defined like most Western Establishments; i.e. acquisitive, profit-oriented, committed to the benefits of technology. The era of the great clerics and of the rural Notables in Quebec was gone. The seventies came under technocratic rule: that of the Liberal party led by Premier Robert Bourassa, starting with his election to office in 1970 with the promise of 100,000 jobs within the first months of his term.

A "brains trust" --along the Ford Company "whizkids"-- envisaged for Quebec an essentially American model for growth and affluence. An uncritical welcome was extended to the multinationals and to theories of unlimited growth. If Jean Lesage led Quebec in 1960 on a "Quiet Revolution" in the direction of a goal which logically forced the *Parti Pris* intellectuals to call for an unconditional "unquiet revolution," Robert Bourassa lay claim in 1970 to the model of the affluent society defined by John Kenneth Galbraith: a society based no longer on national values or on historical demands, but one that recognized only the imperatives of the mass worldwide market economy. Room was to be made for the multinationals and other international corporations. In the span of ten years, from 1960 to 1970, the evolution of Quebec had come full circle. Maurice

Duplessis died in 1959 while visiting the installations of an American mining company in northern Quebec; in 1970, Bourassa celebrated the opening of Quebec to the world by dining with David Rockefeller.

* * *

Indeed, Quebec discovered its Americanness. The popular arts replaced the cultural constructs and concepts of previous generations, whether of the *Cité Libre* or the *Parti Pris* stamp, found to be elitists and in any case "irrelevant." The post-*Parti Pris* creative writers sought to explore further the premises of art rooted in the spoken form of language by making full use of the vernacular of the Montreal east end, "joual" (fractured French). The new populist arts triumphed not in the traditional literary genres such as fiction and poetry, but in the songs and the plays of the early nineteen seventies. The premise of the need to describe the *Québécois* in as realistic a mode as possible led to the celebration (in the plays of Michel Tremblay, for instance) of individuals from the working-class. The accent was on the environment, language, values and outlook of urban street culture deemed to be more representative of the true Quebec reality beyond ideology and political aspiration. The native land was no longer claimed in the lyrical and transcendent fashion of the sixties, but in its quotidian form void of any theory, in drama and the new film industry. It was as if at the end of *Parti Pris* ideology was the discovery of an everyday lifestyle which beyond language did not differentiate Quebec from the general North American mainstream. Which was precisely the theme of a well-known song by the new, "hip" singer Robert Charlebois:"Vivre en ce pays, c'est comme vivre aux Etats-Unis" (*Living in this country is like living in the United States*).

The thinking of the seventies reflected the consciousness of the decisive influence of the media on society. So that, in Quebec as elsewhere in North America and Europe, the perception involved the "generation gap," the rebellion against middle-class values, the refusal of the culture of the academies, the desire for an alternative lifestyle that no political doctrine could circumscribe; in short, the ambivalence of a well-fed younger generation *vis-à-vis* the values of the affluent society. Unsurprisingly, the bible of American youth, Charles Reich's

The Greening of America, was widely read in Quebec; something like "California Dreamin' " became the common dream of many an urban young *Québécois*.

From 1960 to 1970, a new middle-class reigned in Quebec, the product of urbanization and technology. Its values were endemic. There was little inclination for traditional nationalist debates, but a strong desire to correspond to the image of the middle-class in all industrialized societies. The taste was for prosperity, comfort, tourism, the "sweet life." At a time when the *Québécois* could afford to travel extensively; when Quebec industry, whether in the book trade, cinema or hostelry, was expanding, necessitating wider outside markets; at a time when Quebec society was discovering a vocation for leadership of the francophone world; when Quebec had disenfranchised itself both of the "state of siege" mentality of the Duplessis era and of a Third World-inspired ideology, the opening of Quebec to the world meant a new image of self, or the need for a new image of self. But which one? The image of the *Québécois* as a "white nigger" had lost its shock value.

Quebec literature of the seventies indicated, if anything, the end of movements and ideologies. Writers were involved in projects where the imagination was deemed to be self-sufficient. Godbout's novel, *D'Amour, P.Q.* (1972), was a reflection on the impact of the media on modern life; Aquin's *Neige noire* (1974) a mixture of media, time and space; Langevin's *L'Elan d'Amérique* (1972) dramatized the Americanness of modern Quebec; Carrier's *Il est par là le soleil* (1970), *Le 2000e étage* (1973) presented a mythology based on the Rabelaisian grotesque. Poets found themselves taking a back seat. Since 1968, a society moved from a state of uncertainty and ambiguity to one of total openness to all winds and currents. A hitherto intensely homogeneous society moved to pluralist openness informed by the spirit of individual pursuit of happiness of most consumer societies.

Ironically, Quebec and the Third World mirrored each other once more. The images reflected were those of a new middle-class satisfied with itself and bent on maintaining newly-acquired privileges. The landscape was one of sharp contrasts. In Quebec, the traditional elite was replaced by an elite indifferent to the "national question." Where that elite demonstrated a national preoccupation, it was to the extent that the national interest did not detract from the new economic order it benefited from.

Therein lay the paradox of the *Parti Québécois* whose clientèle up to the November 1976 elections was --next to the ethnic emotions and resentments of working-class malcontents given an axe to grind by fanning their nationalist feellings-- drawn from the ranks of this new urban elite produced since the 1960 "Quiet Revolution." And there lay the dilemma faced by the *Parti Québécois* once it rose to power [up to the April 2003 elections when it was defeated for the second time since 1976 by the Liberal Party. Author's note]: how to reconcile the benefits of affluence for all with political sovereignty? How to bring to fruition aspirations to self-determination without disturbing the economic climate needed for affluence?

* * *

In the meantime (pre-November 1976), the vocation of the new elite was illustrated in various forms. It was the vision of the mayor of Montreal to inscribe his city in the lineage of the major urban centres of North America. It was the vision of Premier Bourassa, continuing in the footsteps of Premier Duplessis when he handed over large chunks of Quebec's forests to I.T.T. Or it was Premier Bourassa hastening the coming of a "brave new world" when, in disregard of ecology and the rights of the native populations he launched the billion-dollar hydroelectric James Bay project on Quebec's north shore. No doubt the guiding principle was growth at all cost, at a time when limits were being placed on such a notion in the United States, where this concept had showed its worst excesses. It was ironic that at a time when American cultural influences were rampant in Quebec no one in government seemed to be paying much attention to the findings of a Barry Commoner or a Paul Erlich.

Social inequities meanwhile worsened. Citizens' groups made a dent in the municipal political structure of Montreal, but not to the extent of preventing the wastage that went into making Montreal the host for the 1976 Olympics. Agitation on the labor scene came to a head when labor leaders threatened, in

1972, to bring down the State. They were consequently locked up. Junior colleges and universities jumped on the bandwagon of prolonged strikes. When the November 1976 elections took place, two large universities, one in Montreal, the other in Quebec city, were on strike. But all in all, the consensus was that these turmoils were at best mere reflections of the fact that Quebec had become an open society no different from American and other mass societies. Quebec was in the mainstream of a world order where technology and industrialization were allowed to chart their own course, while, on the other hand, social needs were left attended by rhetorical agitation.

The Third World reflected a similar ambivalence. The state of things in general, in Black Africa, in the post-independence era was that of societies for which the need for a new order had been proclaimed, but which, shortly after independence was achieved, repeated the mistakes, errors and built-in inequities bequeathed by the former colonizing nations. These nominally "independent" societies found themselves still subjected to the markets of Western nations, dependent on their technical assistance, accepting the principle of foreign investment as a *sine qua non* for progress. Briefly, the acceptance of the maintenance of foreign, social and cultural structures explained the existence of an elite whose values, outlook and interests were in most cases merely the mirror image of the former colonizers'. Frantz Fanon had, in 1961, foreseen the ravages of neo-colonialism when political independence was not paralleled by a revamping of the economic structures of the former colonies:

> The national middle class which takes over power at the end of the colonial regime is an underdeveloped middle class. It has practically no economic power, and in any case it is in no way commensurate with the bourgeoisie of the mother country which it hopes to replace. In its narcissism, the national middle class is easily convinced that it can advantageously replace the middle class of the mother country. But the same independence which literally drives it into a corner will give rise within its ranks to catastrophic reactions, and will oblige it to send out frenzied appeals for help to the former mother country.... Neither financiers nor industrial magnates are to be found within this national middle class. The national bourgeoisie of underdeveloped countries is not engaged in production, nor in invention, nor building, nor labor; it is completely canalized into activities of the intermediary type. Its innermost vocation seems to be to keep in the running and

to be part of the racket. (*The Wretched of the Earth* 149-150)

In the Third World, as in Quebec, the population was left waiting for promised rewards like the characters in Samuel Beckett's *Waiting for Godot*. The gap was wide and growing increasingly wider between the standard of living shared by a westernized elite and that of the general population. In the Third World, as in Quebec, the cornerstone of the social order was not so much national as a-national; "culture" simply meant the vagaries of everyday living subjected to the rise and fall of the Dow-Jones average.

Such was the general picture in Quebec on the eve of the 15 November 1976 elections. During the relatively short time span of two decades, a society had been tested by its ruling intellectual and cultural elite against three models. In the fifties, the *Cité Libre* group called for a European liberal and humanist view of man whose primary concern was the preservation of individual rights. In the sixties, the *Parti Pris* people looked to the Third World for inspiration and proposed an ideology for political liberation with the accent put on nationalism and group consciousness. In the seventies, the Quebec counter-culture as well as the Establishment completed the journey where it had begun, by effecting a rediscovery of America.

Hence the central question faced by Quebec on the eve of the 15 November elections was precisely whether the future lay in the continued acceptance of and indulgence in the "brave new world" of consumerism or whether the quest for affluence was worth the price of relinquishing Quebec's indigenous historical and cultural character. Differently put, the challenge was whether consumerism could be made compatible with nationalism. A positive answer to that last question had been badly thought out by Duplessis. Reformulated by the *Parti Québécois* --building on the breakthroughs of the Liberal Party's "Quiet Revolution's" creation of a middle class cleverly juggling nationalism and consumerism-- the answer agreed upon by a plurality of the Quebec electorate suggested that Quebec might be in the unique position of integrating the apparently incompatible values of nationalism and consumerism in the making of a sovereign State. And *that* has yet to be seen.

* * *

Postscriptum

The people willed otherwise at the polls on the issue of Quebec becoming a sovereign State. They democratically made a clear distinction between the proven compatibility --and profitability-- of a merger between nationalism and consumerism, on the one hand, and the unprofitable risk-taking of sovereignty, on the other hand. Put to the vote, the call for sovereignty was defeated in two referenda held in 1980 and 1995 by the *Parti Québécois* while it was in power.

In April 2003, the *Parti Québécois* was replaced in the governance of Quebec by the non-sovereignist Liberal Party whose "Quiet Revolution," in 1960, initiated the ideological merger of nationalism and consumerism in Quebec in pursuit of a society's aspirations.

The logical conclusion of the Quebec paradigm applied to Cuba is the enlarged focus it brings to the interweaving of nationalism and consumerism in the socio-economic fabric of the Cuban State for the foreseeable future. The price for this merger is the same as in Quebec: a redefinition of the idea of sovereignty possibly glimpsed in the silent and unique language of the Cuban look. What it says, slightly paraphrasing Benítez-Rojo, is that the organic meaning of sovereignty of the land rests on the depth and steadiness of a culture symbolized by the eloquence of a language of the senses that belies doctrine and ideology.

The appended text that follows, the "Declaration on Art and the Revolution in Cuba," inversely demonstrates how doctrinal language applied to the arts is a dead-end. In that 1971 text, I see a yardstick for measuring the damage done to literary expression in Cuba (of which Reinaldo Arenas's example is the most notorious) while the non-verbal arts of popular and classical dancing and music, along with the visual arts, have never flourished as much as they have in the last decades and acclaimed by a world audience. In Chucho Valdés's words, "Art can never live in isolation, because art that isolates itself dies. Art has to feed itself from everything that is happening in order to continue to grow" (*Cuba on the Verge* 130). The achievements of Alicia Alonso's dance company, the *Ballet Nacional de Cuba*, Compay Segundo, Chucho Valdés, Gonzalvo Rubalcaba and other artists in music, photography --such as Alberto Korda's famous picture of Ché Guevara [stylized in neon sign on the Plaza de la Revolución]-- and the films of Tomás Gutiérrez matching the worldwide success in sports of the likes of Alberto Juantorena, Teofilo Stevenson, Javier Sotomayor and numerous other Cuban athletes, whose performances are nothing short of aesthetic, bear out Valdés's words.

It is against such facts that the woodenness of ideology results in destructiveness when the freedom to create is denied to the writer, the primary focus of the restrictive measures of the Declaration. Other artists are relatively unmentioned while writers are targeted for intimidation. In the eyes of the State, writing is deemed to be a dangerous practice because it addresses not simply the imagination or the emotions but also the mind the State aims to control. Hence the record of the State's victimization of writers before and especially in the aftermath of the Declaration is such that even some of its early friends and supporters (e.g. Sartre, de Beauvoir, Vargas Llosa) were appalled. [The very long and very well documented history of the victimization of writers can be found namely in Seymour Menton's *Prose Fiction of the Cuban Revolution*, Reinaldo Arenas's *Before Night Falls*, and Heberto Padilla's *Self-Portrait of the Other*].

Yet, for all of its destructiveness, the Declaration of 1971, whose language is draconian, proves to be hollow when juxtaposed with the extraordinary creativity of Cuban non-verbal art forms which parallel the silent, and eloquent language of the look.

B. **Declaration on Art and Revolution in Cuba**

("Declaración del Primer Congreso Nacional de Educación y Cultura," Havana, April 1971. Fidel Castro, "Discurso de Clausura del Primer Congreso Nacional de Educación y Cultura" [Castro is identified in relevant attributions. *Author*] in L. Casal, ed. *El Caso Padilla*; rpt. S.Menton, *Prose Fiction of the Cuban Revolution* 149-151)

1. Art is an instrument of the Revolution: "El arte es una arma de la Revolución."

2. Culture in a socialist society is not the exclusive property of an elite but rather the activity of the masses: "La cultura de una sociedad colectiva es una actividad de las masas, no el monopolio de una *élite*."

3. The Revolution frees art and literature from the bourgeois law of supply and demand and provides the means for expression based on ideological rigor and high technical standards: "La Revolución libera el arte y la literatura de los férreos mecanismos de la oferta y la demanda imperantes en la sociedad burguesa. El arte y la litteratura dejan de ser mercancías y se crean todas las posibilidades para la expresión y experimentación estética en sus más diversas manifestaciones sobre la base del rigor ideológico y la alta calificación técnica."

4. The ideological formation of young writers and artists in Marxism-Leninism is an important task for the Revolution: "La formación ideológica de los jóvenes escritores y artistas es una tarea de máxima importancia para la Revolución. Educarlos en el marxismo-leninismo, pertrecharlos de las ideas de la Revolución y capacitarlos técnicamente es nuestro deber."

5. Works of art will be judged politically according to their usefulness to

man and society. A work without human content can have no aesthetic value: "Para nosotros, un pueblo revolucionario en un proceso revolucionario, valoramos las creaciones culturales y artísticas en función de lo que aporten a la reivindicatión del hombre, a la liberación del hombre, a la felicidad del hombre."

"Nuestra valoración es política. No puede haber valor estético sin contenido humano. No puede haber valor estético contra la justicia, contra el bienestar, contra la liberación, contra la felicidad del hombre. ¡No puede haberlo!" [Castro]

6. Art and literature are valuable means of training youth within the revolutionary morality, which excludes selfishness and the typical aberrations of bourgeois culture: "Nuestro arte y nuestra literatura serán valiosos medios para la formación de la juventud dentro de la moral revolucionaria, que excluye el egoísmo y las aberraciones típicas de la cultura burguesa."

7. A cultural movement should be promoted among the teachers, emphasizing children's literature and educational and cultural radio and television programs for children: "¿Es que acaso cien mil profesores y maestros, para señalar sólo un sector de nuestros trabajadores, no podrían promover un formídable movimiento literario? ¿Por qué no buscamos, por qué nos promovemos, para que surjan nuevos valores, para que podamos atender esas necesidades, para que podamos tener literatura infantil, para que podamos tener muchos más programas de radio y de televisión educacionales, culturales, infantiles." [Castro]

8. An apolitical attitude toward culture is despicable and reactionary: "El apoliticismo no es más que un punto de vista vergonzante y reaccionario en la concepción y expresión culturales."

9. The rules governing national and international literary contests will have to be revised as well as the criteria for awarding prizes and the analysis of the revolutionary credentials of the judges: "Es insoslayable la revisión de las bases de los concursos nacionales e internacionales que nuestras instituciones culturales promueven, así como el análisis de las condiciones revolucionarias de los integrantes de esos jurados y el criterio mediante el cual se otorgan los premios."

10. Great care must be exercised in order to avoid inviting foreign writers

and intellectuals whose works and ideology are in conflict with the interests of the Revolution: "Al mismo tiempo, se precisa establecer un sistema riguroso para invitación a los escritores intelectuales extranjeros, que evite la presencia de personas cuya obra e ideología están en pugna con los intereses de la Revolución...."

C. Understanding Contemporary Cuba in Visual and Verbal Forms from a Haitian Perspective

by

Marie-Hélène Laforest

Most Haitians' knowledge of Cuba is circumstantial. In literature it is emblematized in Jacques Roumain's masterwork, *Masters of the Dew* (1944), whose protagonist returns from cutting cane in Cuba where he has learned the value of unionized work; the benefits of which he shares with his compatriots to help them out of poverty and class division. Cane-cutting by migrant Haitian workers exploited by ruthless and racist plantation owners in Cuba up to the revolution is an early marker of relations between the two countries. (An earlier one is the flight of French plantation owners to Cuba when revolution breaks out in Haiti in the late eighteenth century. But this is a fact only told in French and Cuban novels, and recently re-told in Cristina Garcia's *The Aguero Sisters*.) Roumain's biblical name for the protagonist of his novel, Manuel, signaled the redemptive role he was assigned to emancipate his people from oppression in Cuba and Haiti.

Subsequent to the revolution, Cuba's image in Haiti was an inspiring model of integration of Haitian workers and their descendants who, in a State decree of gratitude for their unheralded work in the Cuban economy, were granted full citizenship. This fact speaks volumes compared to the relentless tales of their ostracization then and now in the U.S., across the Caribbean, and especially in the Dominican Republic. In addition, the sending of Cuban doctors and aid workers to the Haitian countryside in recent years has buttressed the image of Cuba as a model for solidarity and generosity.

Max Dorsinville's book is strikingly original. It is the first book-length account of Cuba written from a Haitian perspective. He begins with the historical reminder of the Haitian presence in Cuba and he unexpectedly finds its embodiment in a Creole-speaking Cuban, the descendant of a family of cane-cutting workers three generations remove from Haiti. Whether by design or coincidence --not unlike his chance meeting-- Max Dorsinville's evocation of Sixto's life in Cuba is in a nutshell symptomatic of contemporary Cuba's ambivalent socio-historical condition.

On the positive side, Sixto's life testifies to Cuba's benevolence toward Haitians. It afforded him and his family a decent life by way of free schooling, housing and health care, and their being made "respected citizens," in Roger Dorsinville's words. These values no doubt stand in sharp contrast to their absence for the majority of Sixto's erstwhile compatriots. On the negative side, the status of Sixto's family is not different from that of most ordinary Cubans. They are poorly paid, subject to food rationing and restricted freedom while they yearn for the relative level of affluence symbolized by the U.S. dollar they see in the omnipresence of foreign tourists; notwithstanding the goods for the tourists' exclusive consumption in select stores and hotels that, for them, are mirages.

The national dignity proclaimed by the State as the result of the revolution is overshadowed by the collective state of frustration exacerbated by tourism. In the everyday Cuba of minimal well-being and maximal yearning for better living conditions Dorsinville sees a reality doubly personified by Sixto's family. On the one hand, he empathizes with the revolution for having rescued Sixto's family from despair and starvation. On the other hand, he is a witness to the gnawing wound that family shares with the average Cuban when the fall-outs from tourism and foreign entrepreneurship elude everyone but the State. In that regard, Dorsinville perceptively refers to the frequent international conferences held in posh venues for the State's prestige. A similar rationale obtains in what he sees in Miramar, the pre-revolutionary enclave of the very rich in western Havana, now reserved for foreign embassies and entrepreneurs, while families like Sixto's fend for themselves in the dilapidated tenement buildings of eastern, Old Havana.

That Cuba has been forced to resort to measures that baldly contradict its initial goal of a classless, equitable society is no doubt a reality dictated by socio-economic circumstances tied to the U.S. embargo and the demise of the USSR, Cuba's former benefactor and protector. It lies at the root of a paradox for which neither Dorsinville nor anyone else has a solution. (I found the parallels he draws in the appendix section between modern Quebec's ability to mix nationalism and consumerism and Cuba's flirt with the latter original. But the living presence of modern Quebec in Cuba tied to the tourist trade is not likely to open the eyes of Cuba's present rulers to its implications for their citizens' individual rights.)

Dorsinville's approach is not limited to the historical relationship between Cuba and Haiti, or Cuba's socio-economic contradictions. From the outset, it rests on the literary perspective of a journey in search of a renewal of value in language which has deadened his senses as a hard-working academic. His, however, is a Haitian-inspired journey. It is admittedly backgrounded by his involvement with his uncle's work that has wearied him. Yet, in this immersion, Max Dorsinville's memory is triggered by Roger Dorsinville's references to Haitian cane-cutters and the Cuban revolution. He is inspired to undergo a journey of recuperation and completion of what can be characterized as his uncle's unfinished work, since he never traveled to Cuba to see for himself what happened to the "respected citizens" he wrote of in the early days of the revolution. In a way, when Max Dorsinville casually refers to his upcoming journey as "a rite of passage of a sort," he understates the personal and intellectual significance of the experience that will result in the ground-breaking nature of his book.

After living for so long in the intellectual shadow of Roger Dorsinville (he edited and/or translated six of his books into English, in addition to editing and publishing his complete fiction in its original French in a collection tellingly titled "Rites de passage"), Max Dorsinville's journey to Cuba was to be that of a quasi-Marlow set to come to terms with his "double," his uncle. If Haitian literature is somewhat short on "father-and-son" relationships, it can be said that *Understanding Contemporary Cuba in Visual and Verbal Forms* represents in the disguised form of an "uncle-and-nephew" connection an interesting innovation in that regard.

***

Max Dorsinville's journey to Cuba is represented in verbal and visual forms centered by the persistence of the *look*, a mute mode of exchange between him and the individuals he encounters in everyday life in Cuba. He changes from an observer to an active participant as he progressively decodes what is initially a silent language by contextualizing it in Modernism which he finds relevant to Cuba starting with the influence of its best-known, long-term resident, Hemingway.

First, Dorsinville begins his demonstration by comparing the omnipresence of the *look* as a form of communication that includes him (he is constantly told he looks Cuban) with the omnipresence of the official discourse of the State in the media and in public ceremonies he finds to be as repetitive as wooden and at a distance from an organic inscription with the people (ironically suggested early in the book by the reference to Sixto's son who does not know the taste of beef). Then, Dorsinville's argument progresses from an initial recounting of real-life encounters to an analysis of literary works by native or non-native writers who voice in their use of minimalism, understatement and indirect, metaphorical language the real, buried language of the people.

The connection between the contemporary Cuban experience and Modernism is built on the relevance of Hemingway's "iceberg theory" to the dichotomy of the people's silent look and buried language. Dorsinville correctly suggests that the Cuban look is akin to what Hemingway identified as the tip of an iceberg: the one-eighth that is seen, compared to the seven-eights that lie unseen.

Hemingway's influence is not only evidenced in the works analyzed, but it is also commented upon in some of Havana's landmarks. The fact that he lived in Cuba for an extended period of time, and that it inspired his masterpiece *The Old Man and the Sea,* a book that testifies to his incorporation into the culture, are well demonstrated. The linkage between the European origin of Modernism, when Hemingway was a young writer subject to the influences of Gertrude Stein, Ezra Pound and T.S. Eliot, and its adaptation in the Caribbean largely due to Hemingway's influence on writers like Derek Walcott, Edmundo Desnoes and Cristina Garcia is equally well brought out.

T. S. Eliot's influence is also convincingly demonstrated in the writings of Ernest Hemingway, Graham Greene, Pico Iyer and Edmundo Desnoes who identify the ruined social landscape of Cuba with Eliot's image of the Waste Land and the search for a unifying myth when the traditional one of the Virgen del Cobre is displaced (Hemingway), diluted in the sex trade (Greene and Iyer) or simply covered up by the official discourse of the State (Desnoes).

Foremost, evidence of the connection between Modernism and Cuba is articulated in the analysis of Maurice Merleau-Ponty's theories on perception revolving around the senses, and especially the body, with regard to the works of Cristina Garcia. The discussion of Jean-Paul Sartre's concept of self and otherness located in the *look* is made concrete by an analysis of Sartre's book on Cuba as a subtextual illustration of his finding closure in Cuban revolutionary heroes for the incomplete anti-heroes of his fictional works.

Finally, Joseph Conrad's association with Modernism is also cogently argued and a Cuban connection is validated in the number of works analyzed that in one form or another are about the uncertainties of locating the markers of margin and center in the kind of world Cuba is represented, as one among many social sites living in metaphorical "darkness" belied by a blinding "light."

Altogether, the title of Max Dorsinville's book is an accurate indication of what lies in store for the scholarly reader in a variety of disciplines concerned with Modernism, postcoloniality and interdisciplinary studies with a focus on Latin America. It principally contributes to knowledge in all these fields by simply, but eloquently, drawing on salient scholarly resources and demonstrating that the first and lasting measure of proper understanding of a subject like contemporary Cuba lies in the inductive hands-on experience of personalized exchanges between the researcher and his/her subject followed by the analytical decoding of unsuspected implications such as those behind the simple *look* prevalent in Cuba.

***

For me, this book is about Haiti in refracted form. It, too, had a revolution which has been iconized to such an extent that the icon --that in 2004 will be celebrated for its creation two hundred years earlier-- has weighed heavily over the subsequent course of Haiti's history like the legendary albatross haunting Coleridge's Ancient Mariner.

Didn't relief from his fate come from the Ancient Mariner's storytelling, his emergence from silence?

Max Dorsinville's Cuba is not only his filling in his uncle's shoes in a "rite of passage" or journey of completion of his uncle's vision when he actually meets with a Haitian made into a "respected citizen" of Cuba. He has told a story about an unsuspected and more lasting organic relationship between Haiti and Cuba, beyond circumstantial knowledge, as an intriguing "uncle-and-nephew" pairing created by common revolutionary upheavals. Hopefully, not with the same results.

Bibliography

A. *Writings*:

Anderson, Jervis. "Derek Walcott's Odyssey," *The New Yorker* (21 Dec. 1992).

Arenas, Reinaldo. *Farewell to the Sea*. Trans. Andrew Hurley. New York: Viking, 1986.
_____. *Before Night Falls*. Trans. D. M. Koch. New York: Penguin, 1994.
_____. *The Color of Summer*. Trans. Andrew Hurley. New York: Viking, 2000.

Bachelard, Gaston. *L'Eau et les rêves: Essai sur l'imagination de la matière*. Paris: José Corti, 1942.

Baker, Carlos. *Hemingway, the Writer as Artist*. 4th Ed. Princeton: Princeton Univ. Press, 1973.

Banks, Russell. *Continental Drift*. New York: Ballantine, 1985.

_____. *Affliction*. New York: Harper & Row, 1989.

Bakhtin, Mikhail. *Rabelais and his World*. Trans. H. Iswolsky. Bloomington: Indiana University Press, 1984.

Benítez-Rojo, Antonio. *The Repeating Island*. Durham, NC.: Duke Univ. Press, 1996.

Bensen, Robert. "The Painter as Poet: Derek Walcott's *Midsummer*," *The Literary Review*. 29 (1986).

Berger, John. *Ways of Seeing*. 1972. Reprint. New York: Viking, 1973.

Cabrera Infante, Guillermo. *Three Trapped Tigers*. 1967. Trans. D. Gardner and S.

J. Levine. New York: Harper & Row, 1971.

Camus, Albert. *L'Etranger*. Paris: Gallimard, 1957.

Cartier-Bresson, Henri. *Henri Cartier-Bresson*. New York: Aperture Foundation, 1976.

_____. *Henri Cartier-Bresson Photographer*. Foreword by Yves Bonnefoy. Boston: New York Graphic Society, 1979.

Casal, Lourdes. *El Caso Padilla: Literatura y Revoluciòn*. Miami: Ediciones Universal, 1971.

Chamberland, Paul. *Terre Québec*. Montréal: Déom, 1964.

_____. *L'Afficheur hurle*. Montréal: Parti Pris, 1964.

Conrad, Joseph. *Heart of Darkness*. 1899. Reprint. London: Penguin, 1973.

_____. *The Nigger of the 'Narcissus'*. 1897. Reprint. London, Penguin, 1987.

De Beauvoir, Simone. *Le Deuxième sexe*. Paris: Gallimard, 1949.

De la Fuente, Alejandro. *A Nation for All: Race, Inequality and Politics in Twentieth-Century Cuba*. Chapel Hill, NC: Univ. of North Carolina Press, 2001.

Depestre, René, ed. *Poesia cubana 1959-1966*. La Habana: Instituto del Libro, 1967.

_____. *Cantata de octubre a la vida y a la muerta del comandante Ernesto Ché Guevara*. La Habana: Instituto del Libro, 1968.

_____. *Poète à Cuba.* Paris: P.J. Oswald, 1976.

Desnoes, Edmundo. *Memorias del subdesarrollo*. Buenos Aires: Galerna, 1968.

_____. *Inconsolable Memories*. 1965. Trans. E. Desnoes. London: André Deutsch, 1968.

"Desnoes en Casa," *La Jiribilla*. Interview with Nirma Acosta. 89.1 (2003)

<http://www.lajiribilla.cu/2003/n089_01/089_.html>.

"Desnoes, El Hijo Prodigo," *La Nueva Cuba*. Article by Belkis Cuza Malé. Enero 18, 2003 <http://www.lanuevacuba.com/nuevacuba>.

Didion, Joan. *Miami*. 1987. Reprint. New York: Vintage, 1998.

Dorsinville, Max. *Caliban Without Prospero: Essay on Quebec and Black Literature*. Erin, Ont.: Press Porcépic, 1974.

_____. "Quebec on the Eve of the 15 November 1976 Election," *Canadian Literature*. 76 (Spring 1978).

_____. "The Heat of Home: Metaphors of Incorporation in Derek Walcott's Poetry," *Anglistica*. 3. 1 (1999).

_____ ed. *The Collected Edition of Roger Dorsinville's Postcolonial Literary Criticism in Africa*. 2 Vols. Lewiston, NY: Mellen Press, 2003.

Dorsinville, Roger. "The Mad King" in *The Rule of François ("Papa Doc") Duvalier in Two Novels by Roger Dorsinville*. Ed. and Trans. Max Dorsinville. Lewiston, NY: Mellen Press, 2000.

_____. *Marche arrière*. 1986. Ed. and Trans. Max Dorsinville. *A Critical Edition of Haitian Writer Roger Dorsinville's* **Memoirs of Haiti**. Lewiston, NY: Mellen Press, 2002.

Eliot, T. S. *The Sacred Wood*. 1920. Reprint. London: Methuen, 1928.

_____. *The Waste Land.* 1922. Facsimilé. Ed. Valerie Eliot. New York: Harcourt, Brace and Court, 1971.

_____. *Notes Towards the Definition of Culture.* New York: Harcourt, Brace and World, 1949.

Estévez, Abilio. *Thine is the Kingdom*. 1997. Trans. David Frye. New York: Arcade, 2000.

Facio, Elisa. "Jineterismo During the Special Period," *Global Development Studies*. 1. 3-4 (Winter 1998-Spring 1999): 57-78 <http://www.colorado.edu / Ethnic Studies>.

Fanon, Frantz. *The Wretched of the Earth*. Trans. Constance Harrington. New York: Grove Press, 1968.

Faulkner, William. *Sanctuary*. 1931. Reprint. New York: Vintage, 1958.

_____. *Light in August*. New York: Random House, 1932.

Fuentes, Norberto. *Hemingway in Cuba*. Introduction by Gabriel Garcia Marquez. New York: Lyle Stuart, 1984.

Garcia, Cristina. *Dreaming in Cuban*. New York: Ballantine, 1992.

_____. *The Agüero Sisters*. New York: Ballantine, 1997.

Granma. Official daily of the Cuban government. Jan. 20 - Feb. 15, 2003.

Greene, Graham. *The Power and the Glory*. 1940. Reprint. London: Penguin, 1962.

_____. *The Heart of the Matter*. 1948. Reprint. London: Penguin, 1962

_____. *The Quiet American*. 1955. Reprint. London: Penguin, 1962

_____. *Our Man in Havana*. 1958. Reprint. London: Penguin, 1962.

_____. *A Burnt-Out Case*. London: Penguin, 1960.

_____. *The Comedians*. London: Penguin, 1967.

_____. *Collected Essays*. 1969. Reprint. London: Penguin, 1970.

Hamner, Robert D. "Derek Walcott," *International Literature in English*. Ed. R. L. Ross. New York: Garland, 1991.

_____. ed. *Critical Perspectives on Derek Walcott*. Washington, DC: Three Continents Press, 1993.

Harvey, David Alan and Elizabeth Newhouse. *Cuba*. Washington, DC: The National Geographic Society, 1999.

Hemingway, Ernest. *The Sun Also Rises*. 1926. Reprint. New York: Scribner's, 1970.

_____. *A Farewell to Arms.* 1929. Reprint. New York: Scribner's, 1957.

_____. *Death in the Afternoon.* 1932. Reprint. New York: Scribner's, 1960.

_____. *To Have and Have not.* 1937. Reprint. New York: Scribner's, 1970.

_____. *For Whom the Bell Tolls.* 1940. Reprint. New York: Scribner's, 1968.

_____. *The Old Man and the Sea.* 1952. Reprint. New York: Scribner/Collier, 1986.

_____. *A Moveable Feast.* New York: Scribner's, 1964.

Hermann, Thomas. *"Quite a Little about Painters": Art and Artists in Hemingway's Life and Work.* Tubingen/Basel: A. Francke, 1997.

Hirsch, Edward. "Derek Walcott: Either Nobody or a Nation," *The Georgia Review.* 49.1 (1995).

_____. "The Art of Poetry," *Critical Perspectives on Derek Walcott.* Ed. Robert D. Hamner. Washington, DC: Three Continents Press, 1993.

Iyer, Pico. *Falling Off the Map.* New York: Vintage, 1993.

_____. *Cuba and the Night.* New York: Vintage, 1996.

Juventud Rebelde. Official daily of the Cuban government. Jan. 20 - Feb. 15, 2003.

Kirsten, Lincoln and Newhall Bonwell, eds. *The Photographs of Henri Cartier-Bresson.* New York: Museum of Modern Art, 1947.

Lalonde, Michèle. "Speak White," *Ellipse.* 3 (Spring 1970).

Lévesque, René. *Option Québec.* Montréal: Editions de l'Homme, 1968.

Lezama Lima, José. *Paradiso.* Habana: Unión, 1966. Trans. Gregory Rabassa.

New York: Farrar, Straus and Giroux, 1974.

López, Iraida H. "...And there is only my imagination where our history should be." Interview with Cristina Garcia. *Michigan Quarterly Review* xxxiii.4 (1994): 604-617.

McCoy, Terry, ed. *Cuba on the Verge: An Island on Transition.* New York: Bulfinch Press, 2003.

Menton, Seymour. *Prose Fiction of the Cuban Revolution.* Austin, Tx: University of Texas Press, 1975.

Merleau-Ponty, Maurice. *Phenomenology of Perception.* 1945. Trans. Colin Smith. London: Routledge, 1962.

Miller, Arthur. *Death of a Salesman* in *Masters of Modern Drama.* Ed. Haskell M. Block. New York: Random House, 1962.

Minkler, Julie. "Helen's Calibans: A Study of Gender Hierarchy in Derek Walcott's *Omeros*," *World Literature Today* 67 (1993).

Montenegro, David. "An Interview with Derek Walcott," *Partisan Review.* 55 (1990).

Montero, Mayra. *In the Palm of Darkness.* 1995. Trans. Edith Grossman. New York: HarperCollins, 1997.

Moore, Carlos. *Castro, the Blacks, and Africa.* Los Angeles: Center for Afro-American Studies, 1988.

Padilla, Heberto. *Heroes are Grazing in my Garden.* Trans. Andrew Hurley. New York: Farrar, Straus and Giroux, 1984.

_____. *Self-Portrait of the Other.* Trans. Alexander Coleman. New York: Farrar, Straus and Giroux, 1990.

Perez Sarduy, Pedro and J. Stubbs, eds. *Afro-Cuban Voices: On Race and Identity in Contemporary Cuba.* Gainesville, Fl.: Univ. Press of Florida, 2000.

Pound, Ezra. "Vorticism." *Fortnightly Review*. 1914. Reprint. *Gardier-Brzeska, A Memoir.* New York: New Directions, 1974.

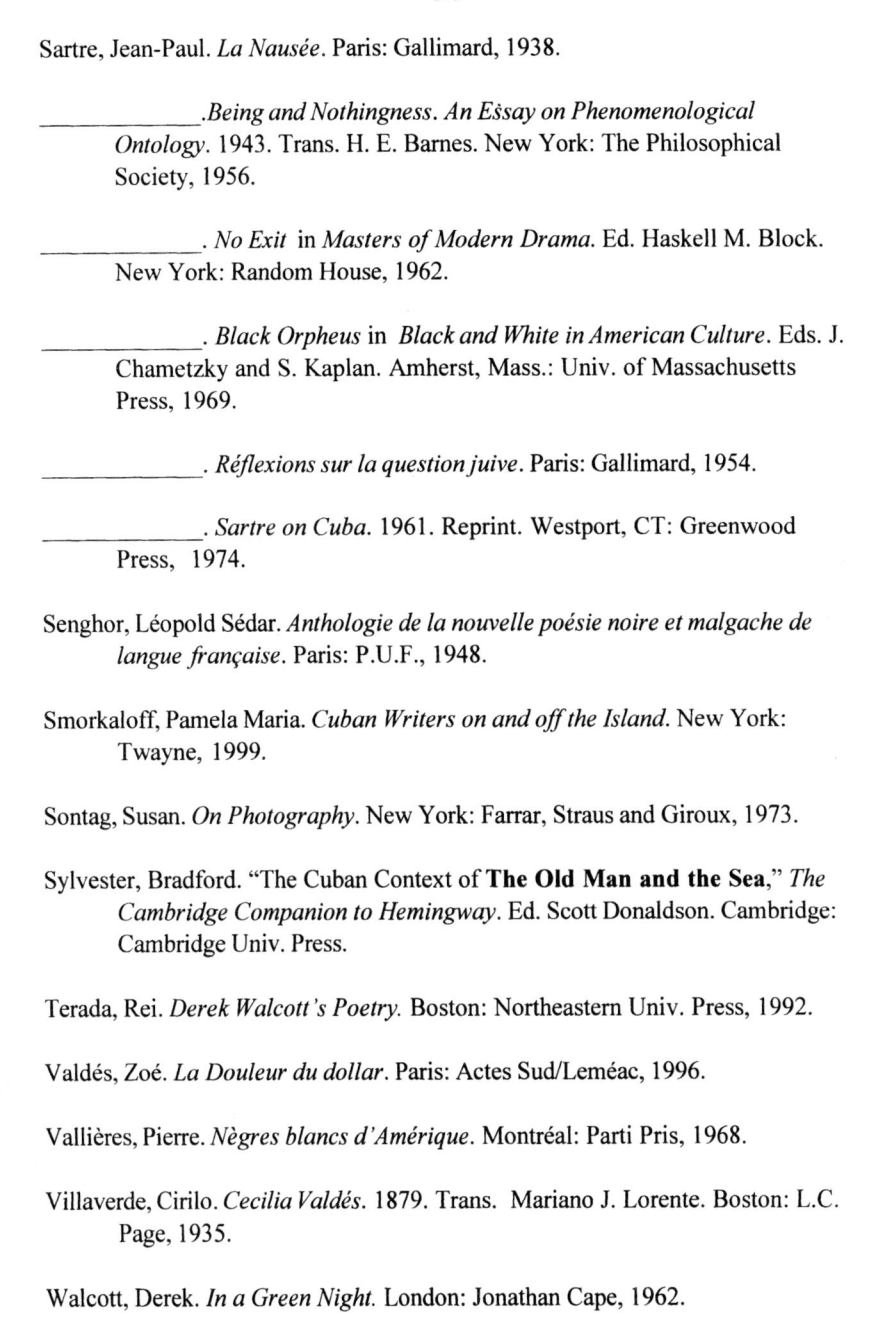

Sartre, Jean-Paul. *La Nausée*. Paris: Gallimard, 1938.

—————. *Being and Nothingness. An Essay on Phenomenological Ontology*. 1943. Trans. H. E. Barnes. New York: The Philosophical Society, 1956.

—————. *No Exit* in *Masters of Modern Drama*. Ed. Haskell M. Block. New York: Random House, 1962.

—————. *Black Orpheus* in *Black and White in American Culture*. Eds. J. Chametzky and S. Kaplan. Amherst, Mass.: Univ. of Massachusetts Press, 1969.

—————. *Réflexions sur la question juive*. Paris: Gallimard, 1954.

—————. *Sartre on Cuba*. 1961. Reprint. Westport, CT: Greenwood Press, 1974.

Senghor, Léopold Sédar. *Anthologie de la nouvelle poésie noire et malgache de langue française*. Paris: P.U.F., 1948.

Smorkaloff, Pamela Maria. *Cuban Writers on and off the Island*. New York: Twayne, 1999.

Sontag, Susan. *On Photography*. New York: Farrar, Straus and Giroux, 1973.

Sylvester, Bradford. "The Cuban Context of **The Old Man and the Sea**," *The Cambridge Companion to Hemingway*. Ed. Scott Donaldson. Cambridge: Cambridge Univ. Press.

Terada, Rei. *Derek Walcott's Poetry*. Boston: Northeastern Univ. Press, 1992.

Valdés, Zoé. *La Douleur du dollar*. Paris: Actes Sud/Leméac, 1996.

Vallières, Pierre. *Nègres blancs d'Amérique*. Montréal: Parti Pris, 1968.

Villaverde, Cirilo. *Cecilia Valdés*. 1879. Trans. Mariano J. Lorente. Boston: L.C. Page, 1935.

Walcott, Derek. *In a Green Night*. London: Jonathan Cape, 1962.

_____. *Another Life*. New York: Farrar, Straus and Giroux, 1973.

_____."The Muse of History," *Is Massa Day Dead?* Ed. Orde Coombs. New York: Anchor, 1974.

_____. *Midsummer*. New York: Farrar, Straus and Giroux, 1984.

_____.*Collected Poems 1948-1984*. New York: Farrar, Straus and Giroux, 1986.

_____. *The Arkansas Testament*. New York: Farrar, Straus and Giroux, 1987.

_____. *Omeros*. New York: Farrar, Straus and Giroux, 1990.

_____.*The Antilles. Fragments of an Epic Memory*. New York: Farrar, Straus and Giroux, 1993.

_____. *What the Twilight Says*. New York: Farrar, Straus and Giroux, 1998.

Watt, Ian. *Conrad in the Nineteenth Century*. Berkeley: Univ. of California Press, 1979.

Watts, Emily Stipes. *Hemingway and the Arts*. Urbana, Ill.: Univ. of Illinois Press, 1971.

West, Nathanael. *Miss Lonelyhearts*. 1933. Reprint.New York: New Directions, 1946.

Young, Philip. *Ernest Hemingway, A Reconsideration*. Rev.ed. *Ernest Hemingway*. 1952. Univ. Park: Pennsylvania State Univ. Press, 1966.

B. *Viewings, Films and Videos*:

Appignanesi, Lisa. *John Berger*. Video recording. Writers in Conversations Series. Institute of Contemporary Arts (1985).

Gomez, Sara. *De Cierta Manera* (1974).

Gutiérrez, Tomás. *Memories of Underdevelopment* (1968).

_____. *Strawberry and Chocolate* (1993).

_____.*Guantanamera* (1994).

Kalatozov, Mikhail. *I am Cuba* (1964).

Lafond, Jean-Daniel. *La Manière nègre ou Césaire chemin faisant.* Video recording. Cinéma Libre (1991).

_____. *Haïti dans tous nos rêves.* Video recording. ACPAV (1993).

_____. *L'Heure de Cuba.* Video recording. La Fete (1999).

Moon, Sara and Robert Delpine. *Henri Cartier-Bresson.* Video recording. Take-Five Production (1998).

Wenders, Wim. *Buena Vista Social Club* (1999).

Schnabel, Julian. *Before Night Falls* (2000).

Trueba, Fernando. *Calle 54* (2001), particularly for Bebo and Chucho Valdés playing "La Comparsita."

C. *Recordings (CDs)*:

Arturo Sandoval. *Danzon.* New York: GRP, 1994.

Beny Moré, *The Very Best of Beny Moré*; especially for "Tratame Como Soy" (I am what I am). Vol. 1. Havana: C.M.Q., 1955-1958.

Beny Moré de Verdad. Havana: Egrem, 1992.

Carisma. Ibis and her band, for "Lácrimas Negras." Havana: Disc, 2002.

Chucho Valdés.*The Latin Jazz Sides.* Havana: Egrem, 2002.

Compay Segundo. *Grandes Exitos.* Notably for "Oui Parlé Français." Havana:

Egrem, 1997.

Gonzalvo Rubalcaba. *Straight Ahead*. Havana: Egrem, 2002.

Homenaje. Chucho Valdés's stellar "El Bolero." Havana: Egrem, 2000

Index of Names Cited

Achebe, Chinua 19

Ali, Muhammad 5

Alonso, Alicia 158

Anderson, Jervis 62, 84, 86

Aquin, Hubert 148, 149, 153

Arenas, Reinaldo iv-vii, 15, 157, 158

Bakhtin, Mikhail 89

Banks, Russell vi

Beckett, Samuel 156

Benítez-Rojo, Antonio i, ii, vii, 2, 13, 15, 19, 24, 25, 58, 120, 121, 131, 135, 141, 157

Benoît, Réal 148

Bensen, Robert 81

Berger, John vii, 19, 20, 22-25

Berque, Jacques 146

Brault, Jacques 148

Bourassa, Robert 151, 152, 154

Bruckner, D.J.R. 62, 82, 85-88

Cabrera Infante, Guillermo iv, v, 134

Camus, Albert iii, 111, 113, 114

Carpentier, Alejo iv, v, 113

Carrier, Roch 153

Cartier-Bresson, Henri vii, 19, 33, 34, 36, 90, 91, 95, 100, 135

Casal, Lourdes 159

Castro, Fidel vi, 1, 3, 5, 6, 17, 92, 105, 107, 112, 114, 119, 120, 131, 134, 135, 139, 159, 160

Castro, Raúl 17

Cervantes, Miguel de 115

Césaire, Aimé 63, 83, 147

Cézanne, Paul 81-83

Chamberland, Paul 145, 148, 149

Chametzky, J. 18

Charlebois, Robert 152

Chrétien, Jean 139

Coetzee, J. M. 19

Coleridge, Samuel Taylor 168

Commoner, Barry 154

Compay Segundo 158

Conrad, Joseph i-iii, vii, 13, 19, 81, 82, 84, 85, 87, 92, 115, 135, 167

"Customs officer" ii, 8, 9, 12, 14, 129

Davis, Angela 151

De Beauvoir, Simone 158

Defoe, Daniel 95

De la Fuente, Alejandro 153

Depestre, René vi

Desnoes, Edmundo iv-vii, 13, 59, 109, 111-122, 131, 135, 136, 166, 167

Dillon, Douglas C. 6

Dorsinville, Max 163-168

Dorsinville, Roger 1-3, 6, 13, 135, 164, 165

Duplessis, Maurice 142-145, 152- 154, 156

Duvalier, François 1

Elena 2, 37, 38, 59, 123-129, 132, 135

Eliel 3

Eliot, T. S. i, iv, v, vii, 86, 95, 97, 99,100,109, 121, 135, 166, 167

Ellison, Ralph 19

Erlich, Paul 154

Estévez, Abilio v

Facio, Elisa 92

Fanon, Frantz 18, 146, 150, 151, 155

Faulkner, William iii, 19

Fernández Retamar, Roberto iv

Fidelito 6

Fitzgerald, F. Scott 19

Frazer, Sir James 109

Fuentes, Norberto 118

Galbraith, John Kenneth 151

Garcia, Cristina iv, v, vii, 1, 13, 20, 23-25, 27, 28, 59, 88, 89, 94, 98, 99, 102, 109, 123, 131-136, 141, 163, 166, 167

García Márquez, Gabriel 59

Godbout, Jacques 147, 149, 153

Godin, Gérald 148

Gomez, Sara 2

Gonzalez, Elián vii, 38

Gonzalez, Juan Miguel 38

Gracia 2, 5, 8, 135

Gramsci, Antonio 146

Granma 13, 93

Greene, Graham iv, v, vii, 13, 95, 101-109, 111, 113, 114, 119-122, 131,132, 136 166, 167

Guevara, Ché 2, 17, 37, 51, 146, 158

Guillén, Nicolas iv, vi

Gumbel, Bryant 4

Gutiérrez, Tomas 118, 158

Hamner, Robert D. 81

Harris, Wilson 19

Hart, Armando 17

Harvey, David Alan 14

Hegel, Friedrich 19

Hemingway, Ernest iii-v, vii, 13, 51, 52, 54-59, 85, 88, 89, 91, 95, 98, 99, 102, 109,111, 114, 116-119, 121,123, 131, 136, 166, 167

Hendrix, Jimi 151

Hermann, Thomas 57

Herrera, Georgina 132-134

Hirsch, Edward 61, 69, 75, 81

Homer 59, 64, 65

Horace 34

Ibis 2, 37

Isabella 2, 5, 8

Iyer, Pico iv, v, vii, 13, 15, 89-91, 94, 95, 97-103, 109, 114, 131, 134, 136, 141, 166, 167

Joplin, Janice 151

Juantorena, Alberto 158

Kaplan, S. 18

Kennedy, John F. 120

Knight, Alden 132-134

Korda, Alberto 158

Lafond, Jean-Daniel 140

Laforest, Marie-Hélène 163

Lalonde, Michèle 148

Langevin, André 153

Laurendeau, André 142

Lesage, Jean 151

Lévesque, René 140

Lezama Lima, José v, vi

Maheu, Pierre 145, 149

Maria 2, 3, 135

Marti, José v, 5, 8, 36, 37, 39, 97, 131, 139

Marx, Karl 20

Maugham, Somerset 95

Memmi, Albert 146

Menton, Seymour 158, 159

Merleau-Ponty, Maurice i-iii, vii, 13, 14, 19, 24, 27, 116, 125, 135, 167

Miller, Arthur 106, 114

Minkler, Julie 73

Miron, Gaston 148, 149

Montenegro, David 63

Montero, Mayra v

Moré, Beny 22

Mukherjee, Bharati 95

Newhouse, Elizabeth 134

Nietzsche, Friederich 19

Nuñez Jimenez, Antonio 17

Ondaatje, Michael 19

Padilla, Heberto iv-vi, 112, 158

Pelletier, Gérard 144, 146

Petrarch, Francesco 114

Pound, Ezra iv, vii, 19, 34, 95, 96, 99, 166

Rebelde Juventud 13

Reich, Charles 153

Renaud, Jacques 148

Reno, Janet 38

Resnais, Alain 114

Reydel 3

Roa, Raúl 6

Rockefeller, David 152

Roumain, Jacques 163

Rubalcaba, Gonzalvo 36, 158

Rulfo 2

Rushdie, Salman 19

Sartre, Jean-Paul i-iii, vii, 8, 13, 17-20, 113, 114, 135, 158, 167

Senghor, Léopold Sédar 18

Schopenhauer, Arthur 19

Shakespeare, William 106

Sixto ii, 2-6, 8, 12, 36, 135, 164, 166

Sotomayor, Javier 158

Stein, Gertrude iv, 166

Stevenson, Teofilo 158

St. John Perse 63, 83

Sylvester, Bradford 52

Terada, Rei 61, 81

Teresita 7

Tremblay, Michel 152

Trudeau, Pierre Elliott 139, 144, 146

Valdés, Chucho 36, 37, 158

Valdés, Zoé iv

Vallières, Pierre 145

Vargas Llosa, Mario 158

Villarreal, René 118

Villaverde, Cirilo v

Virgen del Cobre 52, 58, 99, 167

Walcott, Derek iv- vii, 13, 59-68, 75, 76, 79, 81-88, 98, 109, 125, 126, 128,129,136, 166

Watt, Ian 2, 19, 82, 86

Watts, Emily Stipes 57

West, Nathanael iii, 19

Wright, Richard 19

Young, Philip 57

CARIBBEAN STUDIES

1. Roy Glasgow and Winston Langley (eds.), **The Troubled and the Troubling Caribbean**
2. Anton L. Allahar, **Class, Politics, And Sugar In Colonial Cuba**
3. Clarence Munford, **The Black Ordeal of Slave Trading and Slavery in the French West Indies, 1625-1715**
4. Basedo Mangru, **A History of East Indian Resistance on the Guyana Sugar Estates, 1870-1950**
5. Emily Allen Williams, **Poetic Negotiation of Identity in the Works of Brathwaite, Harris, Senior, and Dabydeen: Tropical Paradise Lost and Regained**
6. Roger Dorsinville, **The Rule of François ("Papa Doc") Duvalier in Two Novels by Roger Dorsinville: Realism and Magic Realism in Haiti**, edited and translated by Max Dorsinville
7. Huon Wardle, **An Ethnography of Cosmopolitanism in Kingston, Jamaica**
8. Roger Dorsinville, **Post Colonial Stories by Roger Dorsinville: In the Shadow of Conrad's Marlow**, edited and translated by Max Dorsinville
9. José Luis Martínez-Dueñas Espejo and José María Pérez Fernández (eds.), **Approaches to the Poetics of Derek Walcott**
10. Sandra Marie Petrovich, **Henry Morgan's Raid on Panama–Geopolitics and Colonial Ramifications, 1669-1674**
11. Leara Rhodes, **Democracy and the Role of the Haitian Media**
12. Roger Dorsinville, **A Critical Edition of Haitian Writer Roger Dorsinville's Memoirs of Africa**, edited and translated by Max Dorsinville
13. Jesús J. Barquet, **Teatro y revolución cubana–Subversión y utopía en** *Los siete contra Tebas* **de Antón Arrufat / Theater and the Cuban Revolution–Subversion and Utopia in** *Seven Against Thebes* **by Antón Arrufat**
14. Roger Dorsinville, **A Critical Edition of Haitian Writer Roger Dorsinville's Memoirs of Haiti**, edited and translated by Max Dorsinville
15. Gray Orphée, **Economic Implications of CARICOM for Haiti**
16a. Roger Dorsinville, **The Collected Edition of Roger Dorsinville's Postcolonial Literary Criticism in Africa: Volume One: 1976-1981**, edited by Max Dorsinville
16b. Roger Dorsinville, **The Collected Edition of Roger Dorsinville's Postcolonial Literary Criticism in Africa: Volume Two: 1982-1986**, edited by Max Dorsinville
16. Max Dorsinville, **Understanding Contemporary Cuba in Visual and Verbal Forms: Modernism Revisited**